Computer Programming
for the Compleat Idiot

for the IBM PC & IBM PCjr

Computer Programming for the Compleat Idiot

for the IBM PC & IBM PCjr

Donald McCunn

DESIGN ENTERPRISES OF SAN FRANCISCO

IMPORTANT NOTICE

The author and Design Enterprises of San Francisco shall have no liability or responsiblity to any person or entity with respect to any liability, loss or damage caused or alleged to be caused directly or indirectly by the information contained in this book.

It is the user's responsibility to test any program, run and test sample sets of data, and run the program in parallel with the system previously in use for a period of time adequate to insure that the results of the operation of the program are satisfactory.

DESIGN ENTERPRISES OF SAN FRANCISCO
P.O. Box 14695, San Francisco, CA 94114

Acknowledgements

I am indebted to the many readers of the first edition of "Computer Programing for the Complete Idiot" who have shared their reactions and experiences in reading and using this book. Their enthusiasm for programming and quest for knowledge has encouraged me to include additional material in the current edition of the book.

I would like to thank Kate Brady, Roxey Drysdale, Lynda Preston, and Jan Venolia for their careful editing of the manuscript and Mark Ong for his elegant design. And I appreciate the cooperation of Paul Robinson and Robert Spaulding of NEBS Computer Forms in providing the art work for the Paycheck and Programmer's Reference Guide.

Last but not least, I would like to thank Tony Leisner, Ernie Williams, and Charlie Winton for their ongoing support of this project.

To Roxey,

    Ruthanne,

        & My Wife

            For Everything

Table of Contents

Introduction

Computer programming is the process of creating a set of instructions that tells the computer how to perform a given task. With the advent of the personal computer, this is no longer the exclusive domain of computer specialists. Now anyone can create programs that will put the incredible power of microcomputers at his or her fingertips.

People have been applying these inexpensive table-top computers to many different uses in businesses, in schools, and in the home. Individuals are creating programs both to run part-time businesses and to make top-level management decisions for some of the nation's largest corporations. Educators, aware that the future of many young people will depend on their ability to program computers, are introducing computers into the classroom for a wide variety of applications. Other individuals are creating programs for personal financial planning and record keeping. And hobbyists have only begun to explore the many potential uses of the computer.

The chief value of the computer is that it can save enormous amounts of time in recording, calculating and filing information, correlating files, and recovering data. For example, simple business transactions, such as the sale of a product or service, result in mounds of paperwork, including sales receipts, invoices, statements, sales tax records, ledger entries, inventory reports, sales reports, profit and loss statements, business tax records, and income tax records. If each transaction is initially entered into the computer, all subsequent information can be automatically generated by business programs in a fraction of the time required to process the information by hand. This tremendous savings in time and effort means that the computer can do for paperwork what the wheel did for transportation.

Some people contend that "computer literacy" should be limited to learning how to operate commercially available programs and not extended to learning programming skills. They argue that a person does not need to know how to design a toaster to use it. This contention ignores the fact that no matter how a toaster is designed, when bread is put in, toast comes out. There is no way to alter the design so that when bread is put in, English muffins come out. On the other hand, the design of a computer program can be changed to produce a wide variety of outputs from any given input.

Commercially available programs are designed to meet the needs of as many people as possible. Yet the versatility of personal computers comes from the fact that programs can be developed to meet the unique needs of individuals. This is important for three reasons. First, the individual user knows better than anyone exactly what he or she needs the program to do. Second, as circumstances change, programs must be altered to stay up to date with the task being performed. Third, an understanding of how a program controls information can help the user discover new ways to use and reproduce that information.

THE ORGANIZATION OF THIS BOOK

This book is designed to show nontechnical users how programs can be developed using simple organizational skills and a minimal vocabulary of terms the computer can understand. It is not necessary to know all the technical details of how a computer works in order to create successful programs any more than it is necessary to know how an internal combustion engine works to drive a car. Therefore, technical information about computers has only been included when it is essential for the development of programs.

This book is divided into three parts. The first section describes the basic operation and programming procedures for personal computers. The second shows how a specific program is used to control the operation of a computer. The third describes a procedure for creating original programs.

Section I: The Computer System

Personal computers are most easily controlled using the programming language called BASIC. This language uses simple English words of five letters or less. The first part of this book describes how to turn on a computer and load this programming language into the computer's memory. After BASIC is loaded into the computer's memory, simple examples show how BASIC controls the actions of a computer. Finally, the process of transferring a program from the computer's memory to Disk or Cassette Tape is described.

Section II: The Program

This section shows how the different parts of a program control the operation of a computer. While programs can be developed in many ways, the basic process a computer follows is to take in information, manipulate it, display and/or print the results of the manipulation, and then store the data in machine-readable form.

The process described in this book divides a program into these separate functions. Each function is entered as a program routine and then immediately used to test the operation of the computer. Variations are included to illustrate the flexible ways in which a computer can be used to process information.

To illustrate the programming process, the specific example of a Payroll Program is used. This program application was selected because it demonstrates the structures of standard routines used in most information-processing programs for entering, displaying, correcting, manipulating, storing, retrieving, and printing information. In addition, the procedure for computerizing the Tax Tables provides an excellent example of how instructions written for human workers can be converted to instructions the computer can understand. And since the government changes these tables every year, this example also illustrates the necessity for acquiring programming skills to keep a program up to date. Variations to this representative program (such as procedures for calculating overtime and bonuses) are provided to show how a program can be modified to meet individual requirements.

Section III: Creating Original Programs

This final section provides guidelines for creating original programs. Standard routines used in almost every program are presented as "building blocks" that can be combined in a variety of ways and adapted to individual requirements. Thus, major portions of new programs need not be organized and created from scratch.

USING THIS BOOK

This book is designed to be both an introduction to programming and a reference for creating original programs. As an introductory book, it can be read from cover to cover. As a reference source, it can be read selectively.

To facilitate the use of this book, the paperback edition may be taken apart and put into a three-ring binder. To "unbind" the book, open it in the middle (about page 100). Pull open the spine and cut through it with a sharp knife. Then pull off the pages one at a time just as you would remove pages from a tablet of paper. After you have removed the pages, punch holes in the paper and insert them in a binder. An alternative approach is to take the book to an instant print shop and have them drill the holes and cut off the spine.

THE COMPUTER SYSTEM

A computer system is a combination of the physical components of the equipment, the hardware, and the instructions the computer follows, the software. This section describes the basic features of these components and provides an introduction to the programming language BASIC.

The physical components of a computer are described first. This is followed by instructions which show how to turn on the system and load BASIC into the computer's memory. With the programming language BASIC loaded, simple commands are used to show how a computer can achieve immediate results on a one-time basis. This is followed by simple program examples that can be entered and used more than once. Finally, the process of storing a computer program is described.

Readers who already have a fundamental understanding of personal computers can proceed to the section titled "The Program."

IBM Personal Computer

Photo courtesy of IBM Computer Corp.

The Components of a Computer

A personal computer contains four basic components: Keyboard, Video Screen, printer, and magnetic storage device. The Keyboard is used to enter information into the computer's memory. Once the information is in the computer's memory, it may either be displayed on the Video Screen or sent to the printer for a permanent record. In addition to displaying information, the Video Screen shows the Operator what information the computer is waiting for or what actions the Operator can activate. Since information in the computer's memory is lost when the power is turned off or when a different program is run, some form of magnetic recording device is used to store the information from a program so that it is available at a later time.

The following description will explain the features of these four components in more detail.

THE KEYBOARD

The Keyboard of a computer contains keys similar to those on a typewriter so information can easily be entered into the system's memory. In addition to these basic keys, a number of special function keys are used to control the actions of the computer. The illustrations on the opposite page indicate the Keyboard layouts of the IBM PC and IBM PCjr.

The keys used for four special functions are particularly important for operating a computer: the Enter Key, the Backspace Key, the Control Home Key, and the Control Break Key, (see illustrations). Their functions are explained below.

The Enter Key is used by the Operator to indicate when a block of information has been correctly entered. For example, if the program asks for a person's name, the Operator can type in Sam Smith. To indicate the name is complete, the Enter Key must be pressed. This key is labeled either Enter or it has a graphic symbol (↵).

The Backspace Key is used to delete the previous character(s) as information is being entered so corrections can be made before the Enter Key is pressed.

Control Home (Clear the Screen)   Backspace

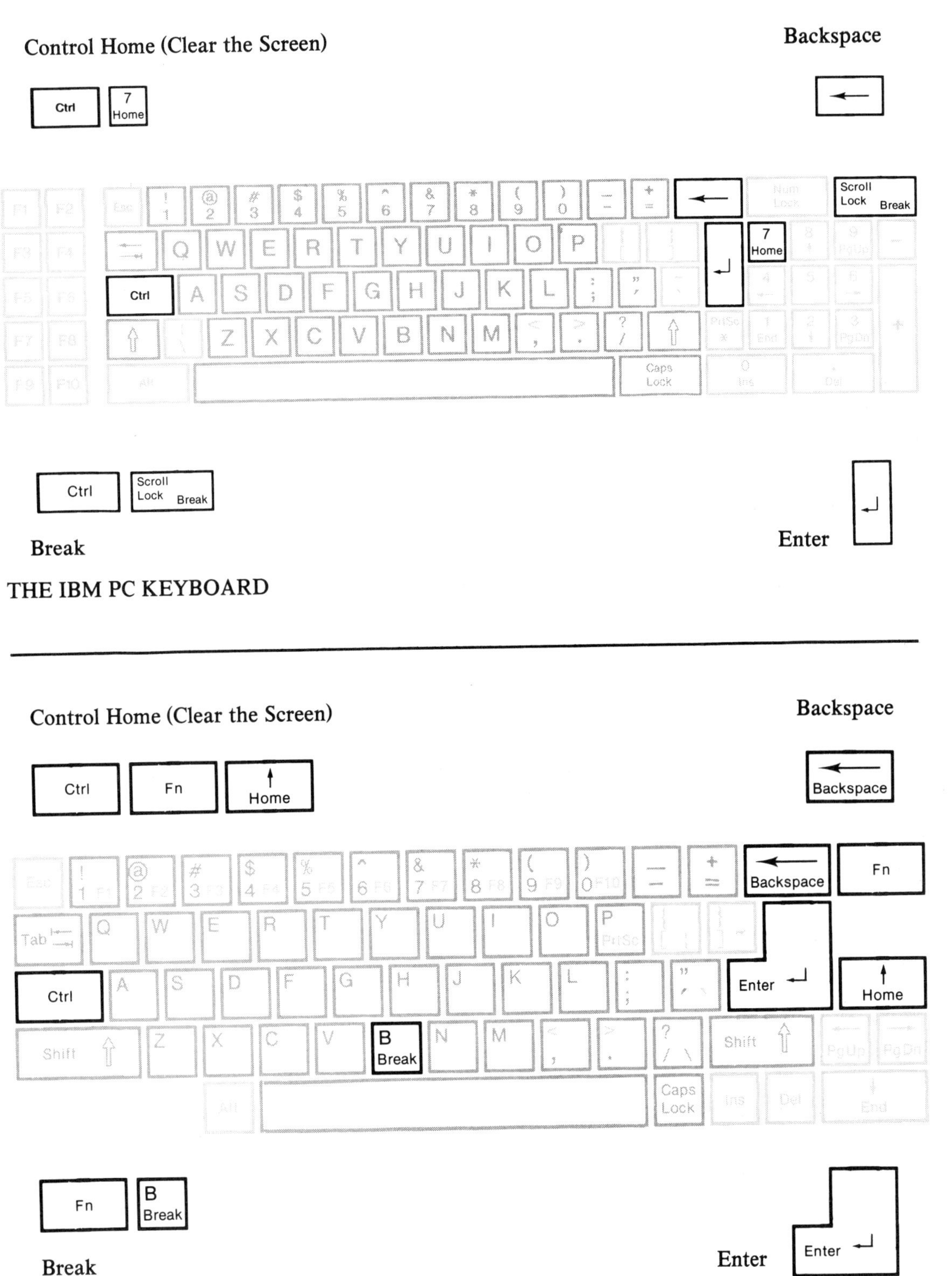

Break

THE IBM PC KEYBOARD

Control Home (Clear the Screen)   Backspace

Break

THE IBM PCjr KEYBOARD

The Control Home Key is used primarily while programs are being developed. It clears the Video Screen of all the information currently being displayed. A portion of the program can then be listed and viewed without extraneous information being displayed.

This function requires that two or three keys be pressed simultaneously. For the IBM Personal Computer, the Control Key must be held down while the Home Key is pressed. For the IBM PCjr Keyboard, the Control Key must be held down while both the Fn and Home Keys are pressed.

The Control Break Key is used to stop the operation of a program. It is primarily used during the development of a program so that changes and additions can be made and then tested for proper operation. The Break function requires that two keys be pressed simultaneously. For the IBM PC, the Control Key must be held down while the Break Key is pressed. And with the IBM PCjr Keyboard, the Fn Key must be held down while the Break Key is pressed.

THE VIDEO SCREEN

The Video Screen displays the information in a computer's memory and the instructions for the Operator. The Screen can either be a television set attached to the computer through a special adapter or a Video Monitor. Video Monitors display information more clearly than television sets because they are expressly designed for this function.

The most important attribute of the Video Screen is the number of characters that can be displayed at one time. The IBM computers display either 40 or 80 characters per line on the screen. From 24 to 66 lines may be displayed at one time depending on the Video Monitor being used. When the maximum number of characters is displayed, information processing tasks are more easily accomplished.

THE PRINTER

The printer provides an important means for creating permanent records of information from programs. Printed information can be scanned more easily than records on a Video Screen. It can also be distributed and referred to by people who do not have access to a computer.

The two main types of printers used with computers today are Dot Matrix and Daisywheel. Dot Matrix printers are usually faster and less expensive than Daisywheel, but the characters are not as legible. Daisywheel printers create copy that is equivalent to the quality of print produced by a typewriter.

MAGNETIC STORAGE DEVICES

The magnetic storage device is an important part of a computer system. It is used to record both programs and information in a form that can be read by a computer over an extended period of time.

The key to a computer's versatility is that programs and information recorded in its memory can easily be erased. This allows the computer to run an infinite number of programs and to record new information each time.

This means that each time a program is created, it should be saved on the storage device. The same is true for any information created by a program. Without this ability to record, a computer's usefulness would be severely limited.

Personal computers use three basic types of magnetic storage devices: Cassette Tape Recorders, Flexible Disk Drives, and Hard Disk Drives.

Cassette Tape Recorders are the least expensive, but they are also the slowest. However, if a computer is purchased to learn about programming and extensive information processing is not required, the Cassette Tape Recorder is a viable option. This is particularly true when a system can be upgraded from a Cassette Tape Recorder to a Disk Drive at a later time.

Flexible Disk Drives are the most popular form of storage device for personal computers because they strike a balance between cost and speed. IBM Computers use 5-1/4-inch Disk Drives.

Hard Disk Drives are the most expensive form of magnetic storage device, but they also store the most information and are considerably faster than Flexible Disk Drives. A Hard Disk system usually also includes a Flexible Disk Drive to make backup copies of the programs and information stored on the Hard Disk.

Computer systems using Disk Drives require special software called the Disk Operating System or DOS. This software controls how the computer records information on the Disk. Special utility programs included with DOS perform functions such as duplicating the contents of one Disk onto a second Disk, displaying the contents of the current Disk, and indicating the amount of room left on the Disk for additional programs and information.

Turning On the Computer

The first step in understanding how to program a computer is to learn the basic operating procedures. The best way to learn the operating procedures is to sit down at a computer and run it. This chapter will describe how to turn on the computer and load the programming language BASIC into the computer's memory.

The procedure for turning on a computer and loading BASIC varies depending on whether a Cassette Tape Recorder or a Disk Drive system is used.

The IBM PC Cassette System

The following instructions describe how to turn on the IBM PC and IBM PCjr for operation with a Cassette Tape Recorder.

1. Turn on the computer using the on/off switch. This switch on the IBM PC is located at the back of the right side of the computer. For the IBM PCjr, the switch is on the left side of the back of the computer.

When the following display appears, the computer is ready to be used.

```
IBM PCjr Cassette Tape System.   The Initial Display:

The IBM PC jr BASIC
Version J1.00
Copyright IBM Corp. 1981,1982,1983


60130 Bytes free


OK


_
```

The IBM PC Disk System

The following instructions describe how to turn on the IBM PC and IBM PCjr for operation with a Disk Drive system. In order to follow these instructions, a copy of the IBM DOS Disk is required. The IBM DOS Disk comes in four versions — 1.0, 1.1, 2.0, and 2.1.

1. Place a copy of the IBM DOS Disk in the Disk Drive and close the Disk Drive flap.

2. Turn on the computer using the on/off switch. For the IBM PC, this switch is located at the back of the right side of the computer. For the IBM PCjr, this switch is located at the left side of the back of the computer.

3. When the date is requested, type in the current date and press the Enter Key.

4. When the time is requested, type in the correct time and press the Enter Key or simply press the Enter Key. (DOS 1.0 does not request this information.)

When the following display appears, the computer is in the Disk Operating mode.

```
IBM PC Disk Drive System.   The Initial DOS 2.1 Display:

Current date is Tue 1 – 01 – 1980
Enter New Date: 10 – 1 – 1984
Current time is 0:02:02.53
Enter new time:

The IBM Personal Computer DOS
Version 2.10 (C)Copyright IBM Corp 1981, 1982, 1983

A> _
```

5. To load BASIC into the computer's memory, type BASIC and press the Enter Key.

When the following display appears, the computer is ready to be used.

```
IBM PC Disk Drive System.   The Initial BASIC Display:

The IBM PC jr Basic
Version J1.00
Copyright IBM Corp. 1981, 1982, 1983

60130 Bytes Free

OK

_
```

Using the Computer

After the computer is turned on and BASIC is loaded into memory, the following tests can be performed. These tests show how information is entered and manipulated in the computer's memory using simple BASIC Instructions.

Typing Copy

Information is entered into the computer's memory by typing at the Keyboard. As a test, type in the word "Hello". The Video Screen displays whatever is typed in. Immediately to the right of the last letter typed is a flashing underscore character that indicates where the next letter will appear. This character is called a Cursor.

Step 1. Type In:
Hello

Correcting Copy

If the word "Hello" is misspelled, the spelling may be erased by pressing the Backspace Key. The Backspace Key moves the Cursor one space to the left, erasing whatever character appeared in that location. The spelling may then be corrected.

Step 2. Press the Backspace 3 Times. The Computer Displays:
He

Step 3. Type In:
xxx

Step 4. Press the Backspace 3 Times. The Computer Displays:
He

<table>
<tr><td style="background:black;color:white">Step 5. Type In:</td></tr>
</table>

```
llo
```

Entering Information

The computer does not respond to the information that has been typed in until the Enter Key is pressed. With "Hello" typed in, press the Enter Key. The computer will display "Syntax error" to indicate it does not understand this particular word.

<table>
<tr><td style="background:black;color:white">Step 6. Press Enter. The Computer Displays:</td></tr>
</table>

```
Hello
Syntax error
Ok
_
```

Computers respond to specific instructions, not to idle chitchat. The programming language BASIC does not know how to respond to "Hello," so it displays what is called an error message.

Computer Instructions

Computers are very obedient about following instructions. But they must be told very precisely, in their own specific language, exactly what they are expected to do. For example, the following instruction will tell the computer to display the word "Hello" on the Video Screen.

<table>
<tr><td style="background:black;color:white">Step 7. Type In:</td></tr>
</table>

```
PRINT "Hello"
```

Once again, the computer will not respond to what has been typed in until the Enter Key is pressed. This allows corrections to be made to any line that has been typed in up until the Enter Key is pressed.

<table>
<tr><td style="background:black;color:white">Step 8. Press Enter. The Computer Displays:</td></tr>
</table>

```
PRINT "Hello"
Hello
```

The computer was told to display the word "Hello", so it did. The quotation marks around the word were not displayed because they are a signal to the computer. They indicate the exact sequence of letters and/or numbers that are to be displayed.

Clearing the Display

The Video Screen can become quite crowded with information. To erase the screen, the Control and Home Keys are pressed. This can be done at any time at the discretion of the Operator.

Step 9.   Press Control Home.

Accuracy

Accuracy is crucial if the computer is to operate properly. The spelling of words and the punctuation must be exact. Human beings can interpret what is meant by a statement if it is incorrectly phrased or poorly punctuated. Computers will not. For example, a program will function incorrectly or not at all if a comma (,) is used instead of a semi-colon (;). The following intentional mistakes will indicate some of the potential syntax errors.

Step 10.   Type In and Press Enter:

```
PRRINT "Hello"
```

Step 11.   The Computer Displays:

```
PRRINT "Hello"
Syntax error
```

The BASIC Instruction PRINT is misspelled in this example.

Step 12.   Type In and Press Enter:

```
PRINT Hello
```

Step 13.   The Computer Displays:

```
PRINT Hello
0
```

When the quotation marks are not included, the computer interprets the word "Hello" as a storage location for a numeric value. No value has been assigned to this word so a zero is displayed.

Step 14. Type In and Press Enter:

    PRINT !Hello!

Step 15. The Computer Displays:

    PRINT !Hello!
    Syntax error

Incorrect punctuation marks were used around the word "Hello" so the error message is displayed.

Step 16. Type In and Press Enter:

    PRINT "Heelo"

Step 17. The Computer Displays:

    PRINT "Heelo"
    Heelo

The computer displays the information included between quotation marks even if it is misspelled.

Numeric Values

The computer treats information not enclosed between quotation marks as numeric values. In this function, the computer can be used like an adding machine or pocket calculator.

Step 18. Press Control Home. Type In and Press Enter:

    PRINT 4 + 5

Step 19. The Computer Displays:

    PRINT 4 + 5
    9

The computer performs the calculation and displays the answer.

Displaying Comments

When a program displays the results of a calculation, it is also a good idea to have the computer indicate the problem being solved. This informs the Operator of the function the computer is performing.

Step 20. Type In and Press Enter:
PRINT "4 + 5 = "; 4 + 5

Step 21. The Computer Displays:
PRINT "4 + 5 = "; 4 + 5   4 + 5 = 9

In this example, the calculation to be performed is placed between quotation marks so that the problem is literally displayed. A semi-colon separates the two items. The instruction ends with the calculation to be performed.

The space that occurs between the equal sign and the number indicates the value of the number. If the value to the right of the equal sign is positive, a space appears. If the value to the right of the equal sign is negative, a minus sign appears. If the two plus signs in the formula are changed to a minus, the result would appear as $4 - 5 = -1$ with no space between the equal and minus signs.

Math Functions

The basic math functions used by the programs in this book include addition, subtraction, multiplication, and division. The signs the computer uses to perform these functions are indicated below.

Calculations are always performed in a very strict sequence. First the computer reads the calculation from left to right, performing any multiplication and division. Then it reads the calculation a second time, performing any addition and subtraction.

- `+` Addition
- `-` Subtraction
- `*` Multiplication
- `/` Division

Step 22. Type In and Press Enter:
PRINT 3 * 5 + 6 + 4 * 2

Step 23. The Computer Displays:
PRINT 3 * 5 + 6 + 4 * 2   29

The sequence the computer has followed is indicated below.

1. $3 * 5 = 15$ (a)
2. $4 * 2 = 8$ (b)
3. 15 (a) $+ 6 + 8$ (b) $= 29$

Calculations with Parentheses

To specify a different sequence, the calculations to be performed first should be placed between parentheses.

Step 24. Type In and Press Enter:
PRINT 3 * 5 + (6 + 4) * 2; 3 * 5 + (6 + 4 * 2); 3 * (5 + (6 + 4) * 2)

Step 25. The Computer Displays:
PRINT 3 * 5 + (6 + 4) * 2; 3 * 5 + (6 + 4 * 2); 3 * (5 + (6 + 4) * 2) 35 29 75

The computer has followed the sequences indicated below for these three calculations.

3*5+(6+4)*2
1. $6 + 4 = 10$ (a)
2. $3 * 5 = 15$ (b)
3. 10 (a) $* 2 = 20$ (c)
4. 15 (b) $+ 20$ (c) $= 35$

3*5+(6+4*2)
1. $4 * 2 = 8$ (a)
2. $6 + 8$ (a) $= 14$ (b)
3. $3 * 5 = 15$ (c)
4. 15 (c) $+ 14$ (b) $= 29$

3*(5+(6+4)*2)
1. $6 + 4 = 10$ (a)
2. 10 (a) $* 2 = 20$ (b)
3. $5 + 20$ (b) $= 25$ (c)
4. $3 * 25$ (c) $= 75$

To keep track of complicated calculations, write out the problem by hand, then draw boxes around the calculations to be performed first. The boxes indicate the location of the parentheses.

$$3 * \boxed{5 + \boxed{6 + 4} * 2}$$

The parentheses must be kept in pairs or an error message will occur.

Integer Values

Another math function uses an instruction which finds the integer of a number. An integer value is the whole value of a number less any value to the right of the decimal point. For example, the integer of 2.54 is 2.

To determine an integer value, type in INT. Then enclose the value to be converted between parentheses.

Step 26.   Type In and Press Enter:

```
PRINT INT(2.54)
```

Step 27.   The Computer Displays:

```
PRINT INT(2.54)
 2
```

String Values

Information contained between quotation marks is treated by the computer as a literal sequence of characters. It is called a String value. When a String value of "1" is added to a String value of "5", the resulting String value is "15", not the numeric sum of six.

Step 28.   Type In and Press Enter:

```
PRINT 1+5 : PRINT "1"+"5"
```

Step 29.   The Computer Displays:

```
PRINT 1+5 : PRINT "1"+"5"
 6
 15
```

Converting Strings to Numbers

String values can be converted to numeric values and numeric values can be converted to Strings.

To convert a String value to a numeric value, the VAL Instruction is used. Type in VAL. Then enclose the String value to be converted between parentheses.

To convert a numeric value to a String value, the STR$ Instruction is used. Type in STR$. Then enclose the numeric value to be converted between parentheses.

Step 30. Type In and Press Enter:
PRINT VAL("1") + VAL("5") PRINT STR$(1) + STR$(5)

Step 31. The Computer Displays:
PRINT VAL("1") + VAL("5") 6 PRINT STR$(1) + STR$(5) 1 5

In the first instance, the String values enclosed between quotation marks produce the numeric sum because the VAL Instruction is used.

In the second example, the numeric values are converted to Strings before they are added. A space appears between the one and the five. This is the space the computer adds to the beginning of all positive numbers.

String Manipulation

Addition and subtraction for String values is the process of adding and removing characters from a String. The addition function is demonstrated in Steps 28 through 31. To "subtract" characters, one of three BASIC instructions can be used, LEFT$, RIGHT$, and MID$.

To create the LEFT$ Instruction, type in LEFT$ followed by the String expression and a numeric value enclosed between parentheses. The LEFT$ Instruction uses the numeric value to count from the left side of the string to the right to determine how many characters are to be used.

The RIGHT$ Instruction acts like the LEFT$ Instruction, only it counts from the right side to the left.

Step 32.   Type In and Press Enter:

```
PRINT LEFT$("123456789",3)
PRINT RIGHT$("123456789",3)
```

Step 33.   The Computer Displays:

```
PRINT LEFT$("123456789",3)
123
PRINT RIGHT$("123456789",3)
789
```

The MID$ Instruction uses two numeric values between the parentheses instead of one. The first numeric value determines the starting position within the String. The second value determines how many characters are to be used.

Step 34.   Type In and Press Enter:

```
PRINT MID$("123456789",4,3)
```

Step 35.   The Computer Displays:

```
PRINT MID$("123456789",4,3)
456
```

Length of Strings

Another useful String Instruction is the LEN Instruction. This instruction determines how many characters are contained in a String of characters.

Step 36. Type In and Press Enter:

    PRINT LEN("0123456789")

Step 37. The Computer Displays:

    PRINT LEN("0123456789")
    10

Variables

A Variable is a storage location in the computer's memory that allows information to be established in one instruction and acted upon later by another instruction. There are two types of Variables: Numeric Variables and String Variables. Numeric Variables store the total numeric value of the information they are given. String Variables remember the specific "string" of letters, numbers, symbols, and spaces they are assigned.

The storage location for each Variable is assigned a specific name. The names of the Variables may be a single letter, a combination of two letters, or a combination of a letter followed by a numeral.

A String Variable is distinguished from a Numeric Variable by the addition of a dollar sign to the end of a String Variable name. Thus, the Variable A is a Numeric Variable but the Variable A$ is a String Variable.

Information is stored in a Variable by typing the name of the Variable, an equal sign, and the information to be stored. The information to be stored in a String Variable must be enclosed between quotation marks or an error message will occur.

The information in a given Variable is "variable" because the computer only remembers the last information that was assigned to the Variable. All previous information is dropped out of the computer's memory.

Step 38 below shows how information can be stored in these two types of Variables.

Step 38.	**Type In and Press Enter:**
	A = 5 : A$ = "Hello" : PRINT A$;": A = ";A

Step 39.	**The Computer Displays:**
	A = 5 : A$ = "Hello" : PRINT A$;": A = ";A Hello: A = 5

Three instructions are given to the computer in this example. The first instruction assigns a value of five to the Numerical Variable A, A=5. The second instruction assigns the word "Hello" to the String Variable A$, A$="Hello". The third instruction tells the computer to print the contents in the String Variable followed by the literal message ": A=", then the contents of the Numeric Variable.

Colons (:) separate the three instructions. In this example, a space is included on either side of the colon to clarify the distinction between the three instructions. These spaces will be left out when the colon is used in other examples in this book.

Notice that the colon included in the literal message of the PRINT Instruction ": A=" is displayed exactly as entered. When the colon occurs between quotation marks, it loses its meaning as a signal to the computer and becomes just another character.

The mathematical calculations that were previously written with parentheses in Step 24 may now be written using Variables to establish the proper sequences for the calculations.

1. 3*5+(6+4)*2
2. 3*5+(6+4*2)
3. 3*(5+(6+4)*2)

Step 40.	**Type In and Press Enter:**
	A = 6 + 4:PRINT 3 * 5 + A * 2 A = 6 + 4 * 2:PRINT 3 * 5 + A A = 6 + 4:B = 5 + A * 2:PRINT 3 * B

Step 41.	**The Computer Displays:**

	A = 6 + 4:PRINT 3 * 5 + A * 2
	  35
	A = 6 + 4 * 2:PRINT 3 * 5 + A
	  29
	A = 6 + 4:B = 5 + A * 2:PRINT 3 * B
	  75

The Variable A is used for all three equations. The first time a value of 6+4 is assigned. In the second case, the value is changed to 6+4*2. In the third calculation, it is restored to 6+4.

This illustrates a very important fact about working with a computer. Any given task can usually be approached in several different ways. It is up to the person working on the computer to determine the specific instructions as he or she sees fit. A program may be judged right or wrong by whether or not it produces the correct answers to the problem.

String Variables may be used with the String manipulation instructions.

Step 42. Type In and Press Enter:

```
N$ = "123456789" : N = 3 : PRINT RIGHT$(N$,N)
```

Step 43. The Computer Displays:

```
N$ = "123456789" : N = 3 : PRINT RIGHT$(N$,N)
789
```

The values assigned to these Variables are still in the computer's memory.

Step 44. Press Control Home. Type In and Press Enter:

```
PRINT A$;A;B : PRINT N$;N
```

Step 45. The Computer Displays:

```
PRINT A$;A;B : PRINT N$;N
Hello 10 25
123456789 3
```

Arrays

Arrays are Variables that are extended to include a numeric value as a part of the Variable name. The numeric value is included between parentheses at the end of the Variable name. For example, the Variables A(1), A(2), and A(3) are three separate storage locations in the Array A( ). The numeric value in an Array name may be another Numeric Variable, A(X). The specific storage location to be addressed in this case is determined by the current value of the Variable X.

Step 46.   Type In and Press Enter:

```
A(1)=5:A(2)=10:A(3)=15:X=2
PRINT A(1);A(2);A(3);A(X)
```

Step 47.   The Computer Displays:

```
A(1)=5:A(2)=10:A(3)=15:X=2
PRINT A(1);A(2);A(3);A(X)
 5 10 15 10
```

In the example above, three different values are stored in the three Variables of the Array. The value in the Variable A(2) is displayed twice because the value of the Variable X is two.

Basic Programming Procedures

Up to this point, the computer has done what it has been told to do on a one-time basis. However, one of the main advantages of a computer is that it can be given a series of instructions which it will repeat as frequently as requested. A collection of instructions used in this way is called a program.

This chapter describes how to enter a program into the computer's memory. Once a program is entered, it may be displayed and modified as often as necessary. The BASIC Instructions used to control the sequence of steps a program follows are also described.

Program Lines

Computer instructions are separated into lines. Each line begins with a Line Number which signals the computer to hold the instruction in its memory and to act upon the instruction when it is told to do so. In other words, computer instructions without Line Numbers call for immediate execution as soon as the Enter Key is pressed, but they will not be stored in the computer's memory. Computer instructions that start with a Line Number will not be executed when the Enter Key is pressed, but they will be stored in the computer's memory.

The computer reads the instructions from the smallest Line Number progressing to the largest Line Number unless it is given an instruction to follow a different sequence.

A program line is created by typing in the Line Number, the instruction, and the desired information, then pressing the Enter Key. The Enter Key stores the line in the computer's memory and returns the Cursor to the left side of the screen so another line can be entered.

IMPORTANT NOTICE

The computer needs to know the difference between numerals and letters. People using typewriters sometimes use the lowercase "L" for a one and the letter "O" for a zero. Computer keyboards always include a one (1) and a zero (∅) on the row of numeric keys. These should always be used when entering numerals. To further clarify the distinction between the letter "O" and the zero, a slash appears through the zero on the display screen (∅).

> **Step 1.   Type In and Press Enter:**
>
> NEW
> 10 PRINT "Hello"
> 20 PRINT "4 + 5 = "; 4 + 5
> 30 PRINT "2 * (4 + 5) = "; 2 * (4 + 5)

The NEW Instruction is typed in without a Line Number. This instruction tells the computer to clear everything out of its memory. Do not type NEW into the computer as a program is being developed or all of the instructions entered will be lost.

Running the Program

The program is now stored in the computer's memory. The computer will not run the instructions until it is told to do so. The program is started by typing in the word RUN without a Line Number.

> **Step 2.   Press Control Home.   Type In and Press Enter:**
>
> RUN

> **Step 3.   The Computer Displays:**
>
> Hello
> 4 + 5 = 9
> 2 * (4 + 5) = 18

Corrections

Everyone makes mistakes. There are two simple ways of correcting any error that has been typed in.

1. Before the Enter Key is pressed, the line may be changed by backspacing to the error and retyping the line.

2. After the Enter Key is pressed, the line is stored in the computer's memory. To make a change, the Line Number must be typed again. The correct line can then be entered.

> **Step 4.   Type In and Press Enter:**
>
> 40 PRINT "So whatt?"
> 50 PRRINT "Don't say that."
> RUN

<table>
<tr><td>Step 5. The Computer Displays:</td></tr>
</table>

```
Hello
4 + 5 =  9
2 * (4 + 5) =  18
So whatt?
Syntax error in 50
```

In Line 40, the error is inside the quotation marks, so the computer faithfully misspells "what" just as it was instructed.

In Line 50, however, the computer's instruction was misspelled so the computer did not know what to do.

These two lines can now be typed in correctly.

<table>
<tr><td>Step 6. Type In and Press Enter:</td></tr>
</table>

```
40 PRINT "So what?"
50 PRINT "Don't say that"
RUN
```

Deleting Lines

To remove an instruction from the computer's memory, type in the Line Number, then press the Enter Key.

<table>
<tr><td>Step 7. Type In and Press Enter:</td></tr>
</table>

```
40
50
RUN
```

Adding Lines

The Line Numbers used to create this much of the program have been spaced at intervals of ten. This is good programming procedure because it allows the program to be changed by adding new lines between the existing lines.

<table>
<tr><td>Step 8. Press Control Home. Type In and Press Enter:</td></tr>
</table>

```
15 PRINT "How are you?"
RUN
```

```
Hello
How are you?
4 + 5 =  9
2 * (4 + 5) =  18
```

Clearing the Display

So far, Control Home has been pressed to keep the Video Screen clear. This function of erasing the screen may be added as an instruction in the program. The Microsoft BASIC Instruction for this function is CLS. However, some Video Monitors may require that PRINT CHR$(12) be substituted to perform this function.


```
5 CLS: REM  Alternate:  5 PRINT CHR$(12)
```

Listing the Program

The program may be run as many times as desired by typing in RUN and pressing the Enter Key. Each time the computer will follow the instructions in the program in exactly the same way. The instructions will not appear on the screen during this time. To examine the program in the computer's memory, type in the LIST Instruction and press the Enter Key.


```
LIST
```



```
5 CLS: REM  Alternate:  5 PRINT CHR$(12)
10 PRINT "Hello"
15 PRINT "How are you?"
20 PRINT "4 + 5 = ";4 + 5
30 PRINT "2 * (4 + 5) = ";2 * (4 + 5)
```

Input Information

The program as it is now written only works with information that is written directly into the instructions. Most programs will require some form of information from the Operator. This is achieved using the INPUT Instruction.

To create an INPUT Instruction, type in a Line Number, the instruction INPUT, and then a Variable. The Variable may be either a Numeric Variable, such as A, or a String Variable, such as A$.

Step 13. Type In and Press Enter:

```
20 INPUT A$
RUN
```

Step 14. The Computer Displays:

```
Hello
How are you?
?
```

The computer processes the instructions to print "Hello" and drops to the next line where it is told to say "How are you?" On the next line, it encounters the INPUT Instruction, which stops the program and waits for the information to be entered from the keyboard. After it receives this information, it will proceed with the rest of the program.

Step 15. Type In and Press Enter:

```
Fine
```

Nothing is done with the information put into the Variable because the computer has no instructions to do anything with the Variable A$.

The demonstration program can be retyped so that it will use the information it receives from the INPUT Instructions to perform the sample calculations.

Step 16. Type In and Press Enter:

```
20 PRINT "A = "; : INPUT A
30 PRINT "B = "; : INPUT B
40 PRINT A; " + "; B; " = "; A + B
50 PRINT "2 * ("; A; " + "; B; ") = "; 2 * (A + B)
RUN
```

Each time the program comes to the INPUT Instruction, a number can be assigned first to the Variable A and then to the Variable B. For demonstration purposes, assign a value of 21 to A and a value of 3456 to B.

Step 17. The Computer Displays:

```
Hello
How are you?
A = ? 21
B = ? 3456
 21 + 3456 = 3477
 2 * ( 21 + 3456 ) = 6954
```

When a number in the thousands is entered, no comma should be used. The comma is a special signal to the computer to read the information to the left of the comma and ignore the information to the right.

Step 18. Type In and Press Enter:

```
RUN
21
3,456
```

Step 19. The Computer Displays:

```
Hello
How are you?
A = ? 21
B = ? 3,456
?Redo from start
? _
```

The error message "Redo from start" indicates that the computer will not accept a comma in an INPUT Instruction.

GOTO Instructions

One of the most versatile aspects of programming is that instructions may be included which alter the sequence of lines that the computer would otherwise follow. One of these Instructions is GOTO, which tells the computer to go to a specific Line Number in the program.

To create a GOTO Instruction, type in a Line Number, the Instruction GOTO, then the Line Number in the program to which the computer should proceed.

Step 20.   Type In and Press Enter:
60 GOTO 20 RUN

This instruction changes the program into a continuous loop. After processing the instructions in the program once, the program reaches Line 60 which redirects it to Line 20. When this is done, "Hello" and "How are you?" are only displayed once. This is because they are displayed by Lines 10 and 15 and the computer avoids these lines by going to Line 20.

Stopping the Program

The program will run continuously as it is currently written. To stop it, the Control Break Keys must be pressed.

Step 21.   Press Control Break.

END Instructions

The END Instruction can be used to terminate the program.

Step 22.   Type In and Press Enter:
90 PRINT "The End" 100 END

IF THEN Instructions

The IF THEN Instructions are another way of changing the direction a program follows. GOTO Instructions always send the program to a given Line Number. IF THEN Instructions may or may not change the sequence of a program, depending on the information that is being processed. The IF THEN Instruction therefore allows a program to operate with flexibility rather than always following the same sequence.

<table>
<tr><td>Step 23. Type In and Press Enter:</td></tr>
<tr><td>

25 IF A = −1 THEN GOTO 90
RUN

</td></tr>
</table>

Line 25 modifies the program so that when the value of the Variable A is given a numeric value of minus one, the program drops to Line 90 which displays the message "The End" and then proceeds to the END Instruction in Line 100.

This function can be tested by entering −1 as the program is running. The results of this response are indicated below.

<table>
<tr><td>Step 24. The Computer Displays:</td></tr>
<tr><td>

Hello
How are you?
A = ? −1
The End

</td></tr>
</table>

Value Comparisons

IF THEN Instructions can be used to compare values in a variety of ways. Step 23 uses a comparison to determine if the two values are equal, $A = -1$. It is also possible to use a comparison to determine if a value is less than an amount, $A < 1$, or greater than an amount, $A > 1$. Using the OR Instruction, the IF THEN Instruction can also be used to check two or more values.

Indicated below is a variation of Line 25 that allows any negative value to be used to end the program.

<table>
<tr><td>Step 25. Type In and Press Enter:</td></tr>
<tr><td>

25 IF A = −1 OR A < −1 THEN GOTO 90

</td></tr>
</table>

The greater than, less than, and equal sign can also be used in combination. For example, the two comparisons indicated above could be written as one, $A = < -1$.

FOR NEXT Loops

The program can also be asked to repeat a specific sequence of steps a given number of times and then proceed to the rest of the program. This is accomplished by using the FOR NEXT Instructions. The FOR NEXT Loop is created by putting the FOR Instruction at the beginning of the sequence of instructions to be repeated. The NEXT Instruction is placed at the end of the sequence.

To create the FOR Instruction, type in a Line Number, the word FOR, and then an equation which establishes the number of times the steps are to be repeated, N=1 TO 3. The Variable N is the counting device. The instruction to the right of the equal sign tells the computer to count from one to three, using the Variable N to hold the current value.

The NEXT Instruction is put at the end of the sequence of instructions to be followed. It will return the program to the FOR Instruction until the specified number of passes is made. After the last specified pass (three in this example) the program proceeds to the next line.

Step 26. Type In and Press Enter:

```
15 FOR N = 1 TO 3
60 NEXT N
RUN
```

The program can now be ended in one of three ways.

1. If a negative number is entered for the Variable A, the program will proceed to the last lines.

2. If three sets of values are entered, the program will perform the calculations and display the end message.

3. If the Break Key is pressed, the program will end immediately.

GOSUB/RETURN Instructions

Functions which will be repeated more than once in a program can be designed as subroutines. The program is directed to the beginning of a subroutine by a GOSUB Instruction. The subroutine is terminated with a RETURN Instruction. The RETURN Instruction directs the program back to the instructions immediately following the initiating GOSUB Instruction.

To create the GOSUB Instruction, type in a Line Number, the word GOSUB, and the Line Number the program is to proceed to for the beginning of the subroutine.

To create the RETURN Instruction, type in a Line Number and the word RETURN.

Step 27. Type In and Press Enter:

```
70 GOSUB 1000
1000 PRINT "This is the beginning of Subroutine A"
1020 PRINT "This is the end of Subroutine A"
1030 RETURN
RUN
```

After the FOR NEXT Loop is completed, the program drops to Line 70. The following display appears.

Step 28. The Computer Displays:

```
This is the beginning of Subroutine A
This is the end of Subroutine A
The End
```

REM and TAB Instructions

REM and TAB Instructions are used to clarify information displayed on the screen.

The REM Instruction allows information to be displayed when a program is listed. It is ignored when the program is run.

The TAB Instruction works like the Tab Key on a typewriter. It establishes the position on the Video Screen where the computer will start to display the information.

To create the REM Instruction, type in a Line Number, the word REM, and any comments that clarify the functions of the program.

To create the TAB Instruction, type in a Line Number, the word PRINT, the word TAB, a number in parentheses, and the information to be displayed. The number between parentheses specifies the distance (in character spaces) from the left margin of the display to the location where the information is to appear.

Step 29. Type In and Press Enter:

```
70 GOSUB 1000:REM  Subroutine A
80 GOSUB 2000:REM  Subroutine B
1010 GOSUB 2000:REM  Subroutine B
2000 PRINT TAB(5);"This is Subroutine B"
2010 RETURN
RUN
```

Lines 70, 80, and 1010 use the REM Instruction to clarify the subroutine being addressed.

When the program is run and the questions for the values of A and B are answered, the program ends with the following display.

Step 30. The Computer Displays:

```
This is the beginning of Subroutine A
    This is Subroutine B
This is the end of Subroutine A
    This is Subroutine B
The End
```

Subroutine B has been accessed from two different locations in the program. First, Subroutine A directs the program to Subroutine B, Line 1010. Then after Subroutine A is completed, Line 80 directs the program once again to Subroutine B. Each time, the RETURN Instruction in Subroutine B directs the program back to the initiating GOSUB Instruction.

Summary

The concepts and instructions described up to this point are summarized in the table below. This basic vocabulary can be used to program a computer. However, a few additional instructions will be added to this vocabulary in subsequent sections of this book. These additions will be used to save and load programs, store and retrieve information, and direct output to a printer. But the instructions already described can be used to create as much as ninety percent of most information-processing programs.

This is not to say that all of the instructions of BASIC have been described in the preceding pages. The IBM Personal Computer has over 185 different instructions that can be used compared to the eighteen that have been described here. The focus of this book is not to provide an exhaustive study of the BASIC programming language, but to show how a simple subset of the language can be used to make the computer a useful and fully functional tool.

SUMMARY OF BASIC

The Keyboard
    Backspace Key   Return or Enter Key   Break Key

The Concepts
    Math Functions: + – * / parentheses INT
    Variables and Arrays
    Program Lines: Line Numbers   Multiple Instructions (:)   Deleting Lines

BASIC Instructions
    Operation: NEW RUN LIST
    Display: PRINT TAB REM
    Input: INPUT
    String: VAL STR$ LEFT$ RIGHT$ MID$ LEN
    Direction: GOTO IF/THEN FOR/NEXT GOSUB/RETURN
    Termination: END

Storing Programs

A computer's memory has certain limitations:

1. It does not retain instructions unless they are assigned a Line Number.

2. It remembers only the last information entered in a given Variable. All previous information is permanently erased.

3. It does not remember information from one run to the next.

4. It forgets all the instructions in a program and all the information recorded in the Variables when the power to the system is turned off.

These lapses in the computer's memory are actually a strength because they increase the computer's versatility. The short memory of the Variables allows an infinite amount of information to be processed through a given program. The loss of the entire program allows an infinite number of programs to be entered into the computer so it can be used for a variety of tasks.

The problem, of course, is that frequently the programs or the information in the Variables will need to be saved for use at a later time. This can be done by storing the data on either Cassette Tapes or Disks.

The procedure for transferring information from Variables to a storage device must be written into the program. This will be described in the next section of this book. The procedure for saving a program that is described in this section saves only the names of the Variables as they are recorded in the program lines. It does not store the information entered into the Variables during the run of the program.

IMPORTANT NOTICE

Cassette Tapes and Disks are sensitive to any kind of magnetic field. Placing a Cassette Tape or Disk near a magnetic field will distort or remove any information that may be stored on it.

CASSETTE TAPE SYSTEMS

The procedure for storing programs on Cassette Tapes is distinctly different from the procedure for storing programs on Disks. For Cassette Tapes, the position of the program on the tape must be established by physically adjusting the tape using the forward and reverse buttons of the Tape Recorder. The best approach is to store a program at the beginning of the tape and use a separate tape to record each program.

To test the procedure for storing a program, the current demonstration program can be saved on a Cassette Tape. Then the computer's memory can be cleared and the program reloaded from the tape.

Storing a Program

To physically prepare a tape and store a program, the following steps must be performed.

1. Rewind the Cassette Tape to the beginning of the tape. Advance the tape in the cassette by hand until the magnetic surface is exposed in the front edge of the cassette.

2. Place the Cassette Tape in the Tape Recorder.

3. Type in the Save Instruction for the computer being used as indicated below.

Step 1. Type In and Press Enter:

SAVE "CAS1:Program Name"

4. Press the Record and Play Buttons of the Tape Recorder and press the Enter Key of the computer.

5. After the program has been stored, press the Stop Button on the Tape Recorder. Some computers will automatically release the Stop Button after the program is recorded.

Clearing the Computer's Memory

It is a good idea at this point to verify that the program has actually been stored on the Cassette Tape. To do this, the program currently in the computer's memory should be erased. The program should then be loaded back from the Cassette Tape. The specific steps to clear the computer's memory are indicated below.

Step 2. Type In and Press Enter:

LIST

Step 3. The Computer Displays:

```
5 CLS: REM  Alternate: 5 PRINT CHR$(12)
10 PRINT "Hello"
15 FOR N = 1 TO 3
20 PRINT "A = ";:INPUT A
25 IF A = -1 OR A < -1 THEN GOTO 90
30 PRINT "B = ";:INPUT B
40 PRINT A;" + ";B;" = ";A + B
50 PRINT "2 * ("; A; " + "; B; ") = "; 2*(A + B)
60 NEXT N
70 GOSUB 1000:REM  Subroutine A
80 GOSUB 2000:REM  Subroutine B
90 PRINT "The End"
100 END
1000 PRINT "This is the beginning of Subroutine A"
1010 GOSUB 2000:REM  Subroutine B
1020 PRINT "This is the end of Subroutine A"
1030 RETURN
2000 PRINT TAB(5);"This is Subroutine B"
2010 RETURN
```

Step 4. Type In and Press Enter:

```
NEW
LIST
```

Loading a Program

The program can now be loaded from the Cassette Tape following the instructions indicated below.

1. Rewind the Cassette Tape to the beginning.
2. Type in the Load Instruction for the computer being used as indicated below.

Step 5. Type In and Press Enter:

```
LOAD "CAS1:Program Name"
```

3. Press the Play Button on the Tape Recorder and the Enter Key on the computer.
4. After the program has been loaded, press the Stop Button on the Tape Recorder. Some computers will automatically stop the Tape Recorder after the program is loaded.

Verify that the program has been loaded into the computer's memory by listing it.

Step 6. Type In and Press Enter:

```
LIST
```

DISK DRIVE SYSTEMS

The location of programs stored on Cassette Tapes must be established manually. The location of programs stored on Disks is determined automatically by the computer. A Disk must first be formatted to the requirements of the Disk Operating System being used. The program is then stored using a File Name. Thereafter, the program can be loaded into the computer's memory by referring to this File Name. A Directory Instruction can be used to see a list of the files on the Disk being used.

To test the procedure for saving a program on Disk, the following steps will be used.

1. Format a new Disk.
2. Save a test program.
3. Clear the computer's memory.
4. Reload the test program into the computer's memory.

Formatting a Disk

Before information can be stored on a Disk, the surface of the Disk must be magnetically partitioned. For the IBM PC computer, the DOS Instruction FORMAT is used to prepare a new Disk. After the Disk is formatted, BASIC and two of the other DOS utility programs can be transferred to the Disk.

To proceed from BASIC to the Disk Operating System, type in the SYSTEM Instruction.

1. Place a copy of the DOS Disk in Drive A.

Step 1. Type In and Press Enter:
SYSTEM
FORMAT/S

2. When the Disk Drive stops, remove the DOS Disk, place a blank Disk in Drive A, and press the Enter Key.

3. Transfer the programs named BASIC.COM, DISKCOPY.COM, and CHKDSK.COM to the new formatted Disk using the COPY command. First place the DOS Disk in Drive A. If a two Disk Drive system is being used, place the new Formatted Disk in Drive B. If a one Disk Drive system is being used, the computer will display a prompt indicating when it is time to put the new Formatted Disk in the Drive. After each line indicated below is typed in, the Disk will transfer a program and indicate when the next one can be processed by displaying a prompt, A>.

Step 2. Type In and Press Enter:
COPY BASIC.COM B:
COPY DISKCOPY.COM B:
COPY CHKDSK.COM B:
DIR

Step 3. The Computer Displays:

```
Volume in drive A has no label
Directory of A:
COMMAND   COM     17792    1 – 01 – 80   12:00p
BASIC     COM     16256    1 – 01 – 80   12:00p
DISKCOPY  COM      2576    1 – 01 – 80   12:00p
CHKDSK    COM      6400    1 – 01 – 80   12:00p
```

Step 4. Type In and Press Enter:

```
BASIC
```

Step 4 returns the computer to BASIC.

Storing a Program

A sample program can now be entered and stored on the newly Formatted Disk.

Step 5. Type In and Press Enter:

```
NEW
10 PRINT "Test"
```

Step 6. Type In and Press Enter:

```
SAVE "Test"
```

Retrieving a Program

To make sure the program has been saved, the program currently in the computer's memory should be erased, then loaded from the Disk.

Step 7. Type In and Press Enter:

```
LIST
NEW
```

Step 8. Type In and Press Enter:

```
LOAD "Test"
LIST
```

THE PROGRAM

A program is a set of instructions that tells a computer how to perform a specific task. There are many different ways to create a program. The approach used in this book divides the job to be performed into three main functions: input, manipulation, and output. Each main function is then divided into additional subfunctions.

For example, the input function can be used to combine values stored by the program in Variables with information entered at the Keyboard. Additional information may be retrieved from the storage device. For the output function, information may be directed to the display, printer, or storage device for later use by another program. Separate routines within a program perform each of these functions. To show how these various program functions can be developed, this section describes the evolution of a Payroll Program.

First the job to be performed is analyzed. Information input is described in two chapters: the first discusses data that can be stored as a part of the program, the second discusses information that must be entered at the Keyboard. The procedure for correcting entered information is then described. A simple calculation shows how input data can be manipulated. Multiple output functions are illustrated, including the storage of manipulated data on Disk or Cassette Tape. Additional calculations are then performed so print routines can be demonstrated. Using paychecks as an example, these print routines show how individual transactions are recorded. To summarize the transactions, a Payroll Summary is generated. Procedures for documenting the program's design are also presented. The program is then modified to create a second program that summarizes the information from multiple runs of the initial Payroll Program. Variations that may be used to create different versions of the Payroll Program are suggested.

The purpose of this section is to illustrate how a task can be converted from a manual record-keeping process to an automated one. The principles described can be used to develop programs for a wide variety of applications.

The Program Description

The first step in creating any program must be to define the job to be performed. This includes the general purpose of the program, the information that must be entered into the program, the calculations and manipulations that are to be performed, and the output that is then required to complete the task. In order to fully understand the requirements of the task, the job should be performed using an equivalent manual system.

The description below defines a Payroll Program used to calculate wages and produce Paychecks. It shows the forms used to record payroll data and illustrates how these forms can be used to determine the required input, manipulation, and output of the information.

General Description

The purpose of the Payroll Program is to calculate, pay, and record the wages of workers paid on an hourly basis using a biweekly schedule.

Forms from Manual Systems

The forms used in a manual system to perform equivalent functions are described and shown on the following pages. The information required to complete them is listed below each form. Note the information that is available before the payroll is processed as well as the data that must be developed through calculations in the program.

W-4 Forms, used when an employee is initially hired, record name, address, Social Security number, Marital Status, and number of Tax Exemptions.

Form **W-4** (Rev. January 1984)	Department of the Treasury—Internal Revenue Service **Employee's Withholding Allowance Certificate**	OMB No. 1545-0010

1 Type or print your full name (1)

2 Your social security number (3)

Home address (number and street or rural route) (2)

City or town, State, and ZIP code

(4) Marital Status:
- ☐ Single   ☐ Married
- ☐ Married, but withhold at higher Single rate
- **Note:** If married, but legally separated, or spouse is a nonresident alien, check the Single box.

4 Total number of allowances you are claiming (from line F of the worksheet on page 2) . . . . (5)

5 Additional amount, if any, you want deducted from each pay . . . . $

6 I claim exemption from withholding because (see instructions and check boxes below that apply):

  a ☐ Last year I did not owe any Federal income tax and had a right to a full refund of **ALL** income tax withheld, **AND**

  b ☐ This year I do not expect to owe any Federal income tax and expect to have a right to a full refund of **ALL** income tax withheld. If both a and b apply, enter the year effective and "EXEMPT" here . . . ▶ Year

  c If you entered "EXEMPT" on line 6b, are you a full-time student? . . . . ☐ Yes ☐ No

Under penalties of perjury, I certify that I am entitled to the number of withholding allowances claimed on this certificate, or if claiming exemption from withholding, that I am entitled to claim the exempt status.

Employee's signature ▶   Date ▶ (6) , 19

7 Employer's name and address (Employer: Complete 7, 8, and 9 only if sending to IRS) (7)

8 Office code (8)

9 Employer identification number (9)

1. Employee's Name
2. Employee's Address
3. Social Security Number
4. Marital Status
5. Number of Exemptions
6. Date
7. Employer's Name and Address
8. Office Code (Employee Number)
9. Employer's Federal Identification Number

Time Cards record the number of hours an employee works each week.

EMPLOYEE WEEKLY TIME CARD

Week Ending ①

NAME ③				DEPARTMENT ⑤		SHIFT	
EMPLOYEE NUMBER ②		SOCIAL SECURITY NUMBER ④		PAYROLL CLASSIFICATION		FILE NUMBER	

DAY OF WEEK	MORNING		AFTERNOON		OVERTIME		OFFICE USE ONLY	
	IN	OUT	IN	OUT	IN	OUT	REGULAR	OVERTIME
MONDAY	⑥						⑦	
TUESDAY								
WEDNESDAY								
THURSDAY								
FRIDAY								
SATURDAY								
SUNDAY								
TOTALS								

THIS FORM MUST BE RECEIVED IN PAYROLL BY ___________ ☐ AM ☐ PM ON ___________ EACH WEEK.	EMPLOYEE SIGNATURE DATE	Sent to Payroll ___________ AM/PM on	DEPARTMENT SUPERVISOR DATE
	SUPERVISOR SIGNATURE DATE	Received in Payroll ___________ AM/PM on	PAYROLL DEPARTMENT DATE

Time Card courtesy of Artmaster Book Co.

1. Week Ending
2. Employee Number
3. Employee Name
4. Social Security Number
5. Department
6. In/Out Times
7. Hours Worked

Paychecks issued to each employee record the earnings, deductions, and Net Pay.

Paycheck courtesy of NEBS Computer Forms

1. Employee's Name
2. Social Security Number
3. Pay Period Ending
4. Hours Worked
5. Rate of Pay
6. Regular Earnings
7. Overtime Earnings
8. Gross Pay
9. Social Security Withholding (FICA)
10. Federal Withholding
11. State Withholding
12. Total Deductions
13. Net Pay
14. Date of Paycheck

The Payroll Summary records the earnings, deductions, and Net Pay for each employee in a form retained by the employer.

		EARNINGS			DEDUCTIONS				
EMP #	EMPLOYEE NAME	REGULAR	OVERTIME	OTHER	SOCIAL SECURITY	FEDERAL TAX	STATE TAX	OTHER	NET PAY

PAYROLL SUMMARY

FOR PAY PERIOD ENDING ① ____________

(The form shows circled reference numbers: ② EMP #, ③ EMPLOYEE NAME, ④ REGULAR, ⑤ OVERTIME, ⑥ OTHER, ⑧ SOCIAL SECURITY, ⑦ FEDERAL TAX, ⑨ STATE TAX, ⑩ OTHER, ⑪ NET PAY.)

1. Pay Period Ending
2. Employee's Number
3. Employee's Name
4. Regular Earnings
5. Overtime Earnings
6. Other Compensation
7. Federal Withholding
8. Social Security Withholding
9. State Withholding
10. Other Deductions
11. Net Pay

Information for the Program

The forms shown on the previous pages indicate the information that must either be entered into the program or produced as a result of the manipulation of the data. The information that needs to be entered into the program can be broken down into four separate classifications.

Information about the Employer identifies the firm preparing the payroll for government records.
1. Employer's Name (W-4 Item #7)
2. Employer's Address (W-4 Item #7)
3. Federal ID Number (W-4 Item #9)

Fixed Information about the Employee identifies the individual worker for both company and government records.
1. Name (All Forms)
2. Employee Number (All Forms)
3. Social Security Number (All forms except Pay Summary)
4. Marital Status (W-4 Item #4)
5. Number of Exemptions (W-4 Item #5)
6. Department (Time Card Item #5)
7. Rate of Pay (Paycheck Item #5)

Input Information identifies the Pay Period being processed by date and establishes the raw data that must be entered.
1. Date of Paycheck (Paycheck Item #14)
2. Pay Period Ending (Paycheck Item #3, Pay Summary Item #1)
3. Hours Worked (Time Card Item #7, Paycheck Item #4)

Information for the Calculations can be identified when the task to be computerized is processed by manual methods. For the Payroll Program, the information for the calculations comes from the Tax Tables supplied by the various government agencies.

Program Calculations

The Payroll Program takes the raw data of the total hours worked by each employee and multiplies this by the rate of pay to determine the Gross Pay. The Gross Pay is then used to calculate deductions.

For this example, the U.S. Income Tax, Social Security Tax, California State Income Tax, and California State Disability Insurance deductions are calculated. Some additional calculations for payroll applications are described on pages 94 to 106.

Program Output

The results of the program calculations provide the information for the Paychecks and Payroll Summary shown on pages 55 and 127. This information is also stored for later use by the program, which creates monthly, quarterly, and annual summaries.

1. Regular Earnings
2. Overtime Earnings
3. Gross Pay
4. Federal Withholding
5. Social Security Withholding
6. State Withholding
7. State Disability Insurance
8. Net Pay

IMPORTANT NOTICE

This is a demonstration program only. Hourly wages are not always calculated on a biweekly period. Taxes vary from year to year and state to state. The principles described here may be used to adapt, alter, and adjust the program to the specific requirements of the user. The resulting program should be run parallel to existing accounting/bookkeeping systems for a sufficient length of time to verify that the program is producing accurate results.

Information Stored in a Program

Information that changes infrequently can be stored as a part of a program. Some examples of this type of information include payroll and sales taxes, postage, fixed interest rates, equipment depreciation allowances, passbook savings rates, telephone and utility rates, property rentals, wages, Social Security numbers, telephone numbers, and addresses.

The main reason for including this kind of information as a part of the program is the speed with which it can be recalled and used. A program with information written directly into it can be loaded and run faster than a program which must retrieve the information from files.

For the Payroll Program, the fixed information about the individual employees is stored as a part of the program. The information can be entered this way when the employee turnover rate is low and wages are only increased once or twice a year at most. Another variation will be suggested later to show how the same information can be stored on Disk for companies which have an employee status that fluctuates more frequently.

To prepare information for storage in a program, the data required should be put into a table that can then be written into the program. When information is entered as a part of the program, a display routine should be used so the Operator can see the relevant data. The data stored as a part of the program should also be clearly identified so that it can be changed as necessary.

Summarizing Information to be Stored

The first step in preparing the demonstration Payroll Program is to create a table that contains the fixed information for each employee.

EMPLOYEE RECORDS

Emp #	Name/Soc Sec	Pay	Mar. Status	Tax Ex.	Code
1	Harrison, James 606-03-7378	5.25	1	1	1
2	Samuels, Barbara 498-27-6249	5.50	3	4	1
3	Johnson, Louis 534-65-1032	5.75	2	2	1

The table gives all of the necessary information about each employee for the payroll calculations. The first column records the employee number that is used by the program to keep the employee files separate and accurate. The second column records the employee's name and Social Security number. The third column records the hourly wage. The fourth column records the employee's Marital Status using the following numeric coding: 1 – Single, 2 – Married, 3 – Head of Household. This information is assigned numbers because the computer can process numbers much more quickly and efficiently than words. The fifth column records the number of Tax Exemptions the employee claims. In the last column, an Employee Code records the current status for each employee, with a value of one recording a current employee and a value of zero recording a former employee. This Employee Code allows the records for the full year to be maintained while only current employees are processed in any given Pay Period.

Storing Information

Information may be stored in a program by using a DATA Instruction. Create the DATA Instruction by typing in a Line Number and the word DATA, followed by the specific sequence of information from the table. Separate each item of information with a comma. Each DATA line must follow exactly the same sequence of information.

Step 1. Type In and Press Enter:

```
9610 DATA 1, Harrison, James, 5.25, 1, 1, 1, 606-03-7378
9620 DATA 2, Samuels, Barbara, 5.50, 3, 4, 1, 498-27-6249
9630 DATA 3, Johnson, Louis, 5.75, 2, 2, 1, 534-65-1032
```

In Lines 9610 to 9630, one DATA Line is used for each employee to ensure that information is entered accurately.

Retrieving Stored Information

The information stored in a DATA Instruction is retrieved for use in the program by a READ Instruction. Create the READ Instruction by typing in a Line Number, the word READ, and then a series of Variables separated by commas. The Variables of the READ Instruction must coincide with and identify the information in the DATA Instruction. The names for the Variables (A,B, etc.) can be anything that makes sense.

Step 2. Type In and Press Enter:

```
9500 READ E,N$,F$,P,M,X,C,S$
```

C	Employee Code
E	Employee Number
F$	Employee's First Name
M	Marital Status
N$	Employee's Last Name
P	Rate of Pay
S$	Social Security Number
X	Number of Tax Exemptions

In Line 9500, the READ Instruction assigns the Employee Number to the Variable E; the employee's last name to the Variable N$; the employee's first name to the Variable F$; the rate of pay to the Variable P; the Marital Status to the Variable M; Tax Exemptions to the Variable X; the Employee Code to the Variable C; and the Social Security number to the Variable S$. Notice that the employee's first and last name and Social Security number are the only three items of information assigned to String Variables. All of the other information is assigned to Numeric Variables.

Information Retrieval as a Subroutine

The information about the employees will be used frequently throughout the program. The READ Instruction that recovers this data is therefore used as a subroutine.

Step 3. Type In and Press Enter:

```
2570 GOSUB 9500:REM   Retrieve Employee Information
9500 READ E,N$,F$,P,M,X,C,S$
9510 RETURN
```

Line 2570 uses the GOSUB Instruction to direct the program to the subroutine starting at Line 9500.

Line 9500 is repeated here from Step 2. After the READ Instruction has been processed, the program proceeds to Line 9510.

Line 9510 directs the program back to the originating GOSUB Instruction in Line 2570 where the REM Instruction is executed. No action is taken as a result of the REM Instruction, so the program proceeds to the next program line.

Displaying Stored Information

The READ Instruction will not display information in the DATA Instruction. To do this, a PRINT Instruction must be used.

PRINT Instructions can be used with TAB Instructions which operate like the Tab Key on a typewriter. The TAB Instruction establishes a location on the Video Screen where the computer will start displaying information.

```
Step 4.  Type In and Press Enter:

      280 D1 = 20 : REM  For an 80 Column Screen
      282 REM  40 Column Screen  =  280 D1 = 0
      2530 CLS: REM  Alternate:  2530 PRINT CHR$(12);
      2540 D = 3 : PRINT TAB(D1 + 12); "EMPLOYEE RECORDS" : PRINT
      2550 PRINT " #"; TAB(5); "NAME"; TAB(21); "PAY";
      2560 PRINT TAB(27); "MAR"; TAB(32); "EX"; TAB(36); "CODE"
      2580 PRINT E; TAB(5); N$; ", "; LEFT$(F$,1); ". "; TAB(19); P;
      2590 PRINT TAB(27); M; TAB(32); X; TAB(36); C
      2600 PRINT TAB(5); S$
      RUN
```

      D   Display Counter
      D1   Tab for Centering Display

Line 280 establishes a value for the Variable D1 which is a display tab for centered headings. By using a Variable to control the centering of the headings, these programs can be used with either a 40 or 80-column screen. Line 280 is used for an 80-column screen.

Line 282 shows the variation of Line 280 for the 40-column screen width.

Line 2530 clears the Video Screen so new information can be displayed.

Line 2540 occurs immediately after the Clear Screen Instruction in Line 2530. It displays a centered heading, "Employee Records", so the Operator will be able to clearly see what portion of the program is currently in use. The TAB Instruction uses the Variable D1 to center the heading. The PRINT Instruction at the end of Line 2540 displays a blank line between the heading and the information that follows. The Variable D records the number of lines of the display required for the heading. (See pages 64 and 65 for additional details about the use of this Variable.)

Lines 2550 and 2560 are used to create the headings for the columns. The semicolon (;) at the end of Line 2550 signals the computer to continue the display after the word "PAY" with information from the next line of the program. This allows the information from Lines 2550 and 2560 to appear on a single line of the display.

Lines 2580 to 2600 display the information about each employee. Line 2580 uses the LEFT$ Instruction to display the initial of the first name of each employee. There is no semicolon at the end of Line 2590 so Line 2600 starts from a new line on the display.

When this much of the program is run, the following display appears. Notice its similarity to the original table.

Step 5. The Computer Displays:

EMPLOYEE RECORDS

```
# NAME         PAY   MAR  EX  CODE
1 Harrison, J.  5.25   1    1    1
  606 - 03 - 7378
```

Processing All the Employees

The information on only one employee is displayed because there is only one reference to the READ Instruction. This may be changed by adding a FOR NEXT Loop which will process all of the employees.

Step 6. Type In and Press Enter:

```
600 W = 3 : REM  Total Number of Employees
2500 D = 0 : RESTORE
2510 FOR N = 1 TO W
2520 IF D > 0 THEN GOTO 2570
2630 NEXT N
RUN
```

Line 600 establishes the number of employees in an early line of the program.

Line 2500 adds a RESTORE Instruction to the beginning of the FOR NEXT Loop to ensure that the program always begins from the first DATA Instruction. The Variable D which records the number of lines displayed is set to zero to indicate no information has been processed.

Lines 2510 and 2630 establish a FOR NEXT Loop for the employees. The FOR NEXT Loop for the employees is used in several parts of the program. By using the Variable W to record the total number of employees, only one line, Line 600, needs to be changed when new employees are added.

When this much of the program is run, the following display appears. Notice that all of the employees are displayed now.

Step 7. The Computer Displays:

EMPLOYEE RECORDS

#	NAME	PAY	MAR	EX	CODE
1	Harrison, J.	5.25	1	1	1
	606 – 03 – 7378				
2	Samuels, B.	5.5	3	4	1
	498 – 27 – 6249				
3	Johnson, L.	5.75	2	2	1
	534 – 65 – 1032				

Controlling the Display

The current program is designed to work with a limited number of employees. If more employees are added to the program, the list may scroll right off the Video Screen so that information about the first employees will not be visible. To compensate for this, the program uses a counter to determine how many lines have been displayed. When the screen is full, the FOR NEXT Loop is temporarily halted. To look at the remaining names, the Operator presses the Enter Key, clearing the screen so the next batch of employees can be displayed.

Step 8. Type In and Press Enter:

```
290 D3 = 24:D3 = D3 – 5:REM  Depth of Display (# of Lines)
2520 IF D > 0 THEN GOTO 2570
2610 D = D + 2:IF D < D3 OR N = W THEN GOTO 2630
2620 GOSUB 2640:D = 0
2640 PRINT:PRINT TAB(D1 + 6);"TO CONTINUE PRESS (ENTER)";
2650 INPUT A$:RETURN
LIST 2500 – 2999
```

Line 290 establishes the depth of the Video Screen in the Variable D3. A value of five is subtracted from the original amount to leave room for the Operator prompts at the bottom of the screen.

Line 2520 is the first line inside the FOR NEXT Loop. It determines if any copy has been displayed, D > 0. If copy has previously been displayed, the program passes to Line 2570 which reads the records for the employees. If no copy has been displayed, the program passes to Lines 2530 to 2560, which clear the screen and display the headings.

Line 2610 occurs after the records of an employee have been displayed. The counter for the number of lines displayed is increased by two, and if the bottom of the display has not been reached, D<D3, or the last employee has just been displayed, N=W, the program passes to the NEXT Instruction in Line 2630.

If the display has been filled, D=D3, and the last employee has not been reached, N<W, the program passes to Line 2620.

Line 2620 directs the program to Line 2640 as a subroutine. Upon completion of this subroutine, the value of the Variable D is set to zero so the screen will be cleared by Line 2530.

Line 2640 displays a message to the Operator to indicate that the display has been temporarily halted and may be continued by pressing the Enter Key.

Line 2650 contains the INPUT Instruction that actually halts the program until the Enter Key is pressed. The program then returns to the initiating GOSUB Instruction in Line 2620.

When this portion of the program is listed, the entire display routine can be seen.

Step 9. The Computer Displays:

```
2500 D = 0:RESTORE
2510 FOR N = 1 TO W
2520 IF D>0 THEN GOTO 2570
2530 CLS: REM  Alternate:  2530 PRINT CHR$(12);
2540 D = 3:PRINT TAB(D1 +12);"EMPLOYEE RECORDS":PRINT
2550 PRINT " #";TAB(5);"NAME";TAB(21);"PAY";
2560 PRINT TAB(27);"MAR";TAB(32);"EX";TAB(36);"CODE"
2570 GOSUB 9500:REM  Retrieve Employee Information
2580 PRINT E;TAB(5);N$;", ";LEFT$(F$,1);".";TAB(19);P;
2590 PRINT TAB(27);M;TAB(32);X;TAB(36);C
2600 PRINT TAB(5);S$
2610 D = D + 2:IF D <D3 OR N = W THEN GOTO 2630
2620 GOSUB 2640:D = 0
2630 NEXT N
2640 PRINT:PRINT TAB(D1 +6);"TO CONTINUE PRESS (ENTER)";
2650 INPUT A$:RETURN
```

Labeling Stored Information

Information stored in a computer program may be altered by retyping the program line that must be changed. New employees can be added by including additional DATA Instructions to the program. Each time a program is changed, the new version should be saved to replace the old version.

The information stored by the DATA Instructions should be carefully labeled in the program. In this way, when new information is added at a later date, it will follow the same sequence and structure as the earlier information. REM Instructions can be used to label the DATA Instructions.

```
Step 10.   Type In and Press Enter:

           9520 REM  –  Employee Records
           9530 REM Mar: 1 = Single 2 = Married 3 = Head of House
           9540 REM Ex: Number of Exemptions
           9550 REM Code: 0 = Past Employee 1 = Current
           9560 REM  Enter Total # of Employees in Line 600:  600 W = 3
           9570 REM
           9600 REM  #, Last Name, First Name, Pay, Mar, Ex, Code, Soc Sec
```

Line 9520 is the heading for the REM comments.

Line 9530 indicates the numbering system used to record the Marital Status of the employee.

Line 9540 describes the Tax Exemptions.

Line 9550 explains the Employee Code.

Line 9560 indicates that the value of the Variable W in Line 600 must be changed when additional employees are added.

Information from the Keyboard

Information that varies from one run of a program to the next should be entered from the Keyboard using INPUT Instructions. In the case of the Payroll Program, the number of hours each employee has worked during a given Pay Period must be entered.

The Variable that holds the employee hours is called an Array. An Array can generate a vast "array" of Variables because each different numeric value placed between the parentheses of an Array creates a different Variable.

For the Payroll Program, the Variable E, the Employee Number, is used inside the parentheses of the Array. This means that each Employee Number creates a different set of Variables. Thus, the hours of each employee are kept distinctly separate from the hours of the other employees.

The Array is processed so that hours for each employee can be entered using an INPUT Instruction. After the information is entered, a display routine is used to show the results.

Entering Information

The Payroll Program described here is for a biweekly Pay Period. The hours for each employee are entered as a total for each week. This allows the program to automatically calculate overtime earnings.

The Array used for the first week is W1(E) and for the second week, W2(E). Two separate INPUT Instructions are used to establish the values for these Arrays.

A FOR NEXT Loop is used to process the full list of employees.

Step 1. Type In and Press Enter:

```
1000 RESTORE
1010 FOR N = 1 TO W
1020 GOSUB 9500:REM  Retrieve Employee Information
1050 PRINT "WEEK 1";:INPUT W1(E)
1060 PRINT "WEEK 2";:INPUT W2(E)
1400 NEXT N
```

Line 1000 is the RESTORE Instruction which ensures that the program starts from the first employee record stored in the DATA Instruction.

Lines 1010 and 1400 form the FOR NEXT Loop which processes the INPUT Instructions for all of the employees as determined by the value in the Variable W.

Line 1020 retrieves the employee records.

Lines 1050 and 1060 are each made up of two separate instructions. The first instruction displays the prompt for the Operator to indicate the information that is required. The second instruction is the INPUT Instruction which accepts the Operator's input.

Identifying Current Employees

The INPUT Instructions do not need to be accessed for employees who are no longer working for the company. The Employee Code records this information by assigning a value of one to current employees and a value of zero to former employees. The program can be instructed to bypass the INPUT Instructions for former employees.

A prompt is added to indicate to the Operator the name of the Employee to be processed.

Step 2. Type In and Press Enter:

```
500 CLS: REM  Alternate:  500 PRINT CHR$(12);
1030 IF C <1 THEN GOTO 1400
1040 PRINT:PRINT:PRINT "TOTAL HOURS WORKED BY: ";N$
LIST 1000-1999
```

C   Employee Code

Line 500 clears the display screen.

Line 1030 determines when a person is no longer employed, C<1, and sends the program to Line 1400, the NEXT Instruction.

Line 1040 displays the name of the current employee as retained in the Variable N$.

When this routine is listed, the following lines appear.

Step 3. The Computer Displays:

```
1000 RESTORE
1010 FOR N=1 TO W
1020 GOSUB 9500:REM  Retrieve Employee Information
1030 IF C<1 THEN GOTO 1400
1040 PRINT:PRINT:PRINT "TOTAL HOURS WORKED BY: ";N$
1050 PRINT "WEEK 1";:INPUT W1(E)
1060 PRINT "WEEK 2";:INPUT W2(E)
1400 NEXT N
```

Testing the Entry Routine

The program can now be run to test the initial entry routine.

Step 4. Type In and Press Enter:

```
RUN
```

Step 5. The Computer Displays:

```
TOTAL HOURS WORKED BY: Harrison
WEEK 1? —
```

Displaying Entered Information

The information that has been entered into a program should be displayed to ensure that it is correct. The format used to perform this display routine is the same as the one described for the display of the Employee Records on pages 62 to 65.

Step 6.   Type In and Press Enter:

```
2000 D = 0: RESTORE
2010 FOR N = 1 TO W
2020 IF D>0 THEN GOTO 2070
2030 CLS: REM  Alternate:  2030 PRINT CHR$(12);
2040 D = 3: PRINT TAB(D1 + 12); "CURRENT PAYROLL": PRINT
2050 PRINT " #"; TAB(5); "NAME"; TAB(17); "HOURS";
2060 PRINT TAB(26); "AT"; TAB(32); "GROSS PAY"
2070 GOSUB 9500: REM  Retrieve Employee Information
2080 IF C <1 THEN GOTO 2130
2090 PRINT E; TAB(5); N$; TAB(17); W1(E) + W2(E);
2100 PRINT TAB(24); P; TAB(32); GP(E)
2110 D = D + 1: IF D <D3 OR N = W THEN GOTO 2130
2120 GOSUB 2140: D = 0
2130 NEXT N
2140 PRINT: PRINT TAB(D1 + 6); "TO CONTINUE PRESS (ENTER)";
2150 INPUT A$: RETURN
RUN
```

Only the content of the headings in Lines 2040 to 2060 and the information displayed for each employee in Lines 2090 and 2100 differ from the display routine in Lines 2500 to 2650.

Line 2080 also adds a control that bypasses former employees.

Testing the Display

Run the program now to test the display routine. When the hours for Harrison are requested, enter 43 hours for week one and 35 hours for week two. When the hours for Samuels are requested, enter 41 hours for week one and 44 hours for week two. When the hours for Johnson are requested, enter 28 hours for week one and 35 hours for week two. The following display will appear.

Step 7. The Computer Displays:

```
                    CURRENT PAYROLL

      #  NAME       HOURS   AT    GROSS PAY
      1  Harrison    78     5.25    0
      2  Samuels     85     5.5     0
      3  Johnson     63     5.75    0

                TO CONTINUE PRESS (ENTER)? __
```

The display indicates a column for Gross Pay which will be calculated later, see pages 75 and 76.

Corrections

It is very easy to make a mistake when typing information into a program. Once the Enter Key is pressed, all information, including any errors, is stored in the computer's memory. The following routine allows corrections to be made.

The principle behind correcting an error is to place the exact Variable containing the error back into an INPUT Instruction. The correct value is entered and the wrong value is removed from the computer's memory.

Correcting an Entry

There are two INPUT Instructions for the initial entry of the information, so there must be two INPUT Instructions for the corrections.

<table>
<tr><td>Step 1. Type In and Press Enter:</td></tr>
<tr><td>

```
3530 PRINT "HOURS FOR WEEK 1";:INPUT W1(E)
3550 PRINT "HOURS FOR WEEK 2";:INPUT W2(E)
```

</td></tr>
</table>

Lines 3530 and 3550 contain two instructions. The first instruction displays a prompt for the Operator to indicate the information for which the program is waiting. The second instruction accepts the information from the Operator.

Selecting the Correction to be Made

Next, instructions must be added that will allow the Operator to specify which week is to be changed.

<table>
<tr><td>Step 2. Type In and Press Enter:</td></tr>
<tr><td>

```
3500 WK=0:PRINT:PRINT "CORRECT WEEK 1 OR 2";:INPUT WK
3510 PRINT:ON WK GOTO 3530,3550
3520 GOTO 3500
```

</td></tr>
</table>

Line 3500 allows the Operator to specify the week to be changed.

Line 3510 uses an ON GOTO Instruction to direct the program to the appropriate line where the hours for the week will be changed. The GOTO Instruction uses the value in the Variable WK to count over to the designated Line Number. If the value of WK is one, the program progresses to the first Line Number indicated, Line 3530. If the value of WK is two, the program counts over to the second Line Number and directs the program to progress to Line 3550. If the Variable WK contains any value other than one or two, the program drops to Line 3520.

Line 3520 directs the program back up to Line 3500. If the Operator does not enter a value of one or two, the program will never leave this routine.

Selecting the Next Function

After one week is corrected, the Operator can be given the option of correcting the hours for the other week.

Step 3.   Type In and Press Enter:

```
3540 GOTO 3560
3560 PRINT:PRINT "CORRECT THE OTHER WEEK (Y OR <N>)";
3570 A$ = "":INPUT A$:A = 2:IF A$ = "Y" OR A$ = "y" THEN A = 1
3580 IF A = 1 THEN GOTO 3500
```

Line 3540 occurs immediately after the change to the first week. It directs the program to Line 3560 so a decision can be made as to whether week two is to be changed. If this GOTO Instruction were not present, the program would always go from the correction for week one to the correction for week two.

Line 3560 displays the option to specify if the other week is to be changed. The most frequent response to this question will probably be "No", so the "N" is enclosed between the greater than and less than signs. These two symbols indicate to the Operator that this response can be activated simply by pressing the Enter Key.

Line 3570 accepts the Operator's response. It then assumes the negative response has been selected by assigning a value of 2 to the Variable A. If a "Yes" response is indicated, the IF THEN Instruction changes the value of A to 1.

Line 3580 directs the program back to the beginning of the correction routine when a "Yes" response sets the value of the Variable A to 1.

Corrections as a Subroutine

The correction routine is designed as a subroutine so that it can be accessed from different parts of the program.

```
Step 4.   Type In and Press Enter:

          1070 PRINT:PRINT"CORRECT THESE HOURS (Y OR  <N>)";
          1080 A$ = "":INPUT A$:A = 2:IF A$ = "Y" OR A$ = "y" THEN A = 1
          1090 IF A = 1 THEN GOSUB 3500:REM  Correct Hours
          3590 RETURN
          LIST 1000 - 1999
```

Line 1070 displays the option to select the correction routine. The most frequent response to this question will most likely be "No", so the "N" is surrounded by the greater than and less than signs.

Line 1080 accepts the Operator's response and sets the automatic response to "N" by assigning a value of 2 to the Variable A. If the response is "Y", the value of the Variable A is changed to 1.

Line 1090 directs the program to the correction subroutine when a "Yes" response assigns a value of 1 to the Variable A.

Line 3590 occurs at the end of the correction routine. It returns the program to the originating GOSUB Instruction.

The option to correct the entered information is placed immediately after the hours have been entered for each employee. This can be seen from the listing of the entry routine shown below.

```
Step 5.   The Computer Displays:

          1000 RESTORE
          1010 FOR N = 1 TO W
          1020 GOSUB 9500:REM  Retrieve Employee Information
          1030 IF C <1 THEN GOTO 1400
          1040 PRINT:PRINT:PRINT "TOTAL HOURS WORKED BY: ";N$
          1050 PRINT "WEEK 1";:INPUT W1(E)
          1060 PRINT "WEEK 2";:INPUT W2(E)
          1070 PRINT:PRINT "CORRECT THESE HOURS (Y OR  <N>)";
          1080 A$ = "":INPUT A$:A = 2:IF A$ = "Y" OR A$ = "y" THEN A = 1
          1090 IF A = 1 THEN GOSUB 3500:REM  Correct Hours
          1400 NEXT N
```

Lines 1000 to 1060 and Line 1400 form the basic entry routine that has been described previously.

Lines 1070 to 1090 provide the Operator with the option to change the entered information.

Simple Calculations

The program may now be used to perform a simple calculation using the information that has been entered. This calculation allows the computer to run through the functions of the program, testing each routine in proper sequence. Additional calculations are described later.

Calculating Gross Pay
The Gross Pay of the employees is determined by adding the hours for both weeks and multiplying this figure by the hourly rate of pay.

<table>
<tr><td colspan="2" style="background:black;color:white">Step 1. Type In and Press Enter:</td></tr>
<tr><td>

```
1100 GOSUB 4000:REM  Calculate Pay & Deductions
4000 REM  Payroll Calculations
4090 GP(E)=(W1(E)+W2(E))*P:REM  Temporary Line
4690 RETURN
```

</td></tr>
</table>

      P   Rate of Pay

Line 1100 occurs immediately after the correction routine. It directs the program to the calculation subroutine starting at Line 4000.

Line 4090 stores the Gross Pay in the Array GP(E). It is determined by adding the hours for the two weeks together (W1(E)+W2(E)) and multiplying this by the rate of pay stored in the Variable P. This is a temporary line used to perform this calculation. It will be replaced later by a more comprehensive calculation.

Line 4690 terminates the subroutine with a RETURN Instruction.

Totaling Gross Pay

The Gross Pay for all of the employees can be added together to determine the total payroll.

The principle of totaling the information in an Array is common to many programs, so it is an important one to understand. It is accomplished by adding the contents of every Variable in the Array to a separate Variable used just to record this information. Normally, the information in a Variable is dropped from the computer's memory when a new value is added. However, the information already in the Variable may be used as a part of the formula for determining the new value for that Variable.

```
Step 2.   Type In and Press Enter:

        2005 T = 0
        2105 T = T + GP(E)
        2135 PRINT:PRINT "THE TOTAL PAYROLL IS $";T
        RUN
```

Line 2005 sets the value in the Variable T to zero, so it can be used to accumulate the total Gross Pay of all the employees. This line occurs before the FOR NEXT Loop in Lines 2010 to 2130 of the display routine. If the value of the Variable T is set to zero inside the FOR NEXT Loop, it will not accumulate the total.

Line 2105 is inside the FOR NEXT Loop. It combines the value currently in the totaling Variable T with the value of the current employee's Gross Pay from the Variable GP(E). This combined total is then used as the new value for the Variable T.

Line 2135 displays the total for the payroll.

Testing the Program

This much of the program can be run. When the hours for Harrison are requested, enter 43 for week one and 35 for week two. When the hours for Samuels are requested, enter 41 for week one and 44 for week two. When the hours for Johnson are requested, enter 28 for week one and 35 for week two. After the hours for Johnson are entered, the display below will appear.

```
Step 3.   The Computer Displays:



                        CURRENT PAYROLL

        #  NAME         HOURS    AT    GROSS PAY
        1  Harrison      78     5.25     409.5
        2  Samuels       85     5.5      467.5
        3  Johnson       63     5.75     362.25

        THE TOTAL PAYROLL IS $ 1239.25

                            TO CONTINUE PRESS (ENTER)? _
```

Multiple Output Functions

The Payroll Program follows the same basic sequence of steps that many programs use: information is entered; corrections are made as necessary; calculations are performed; and the results are displayed.

Actually, the results of a given program may be used in many different ways. The information can be displayed on the Video Screen in several different formats. It can be stored on magnetic recording devices for use at a later time. And printers can be used to generate a variety of documents.

Not all of these functions may be required for each run of the program, and the sequence in which these functions are performed may change from one run to the next. Some functions may need to be performed twice if, for example, a printer jams or runs out of paper or ribbon. The Operator must therefore be able to select which function the computer is to perform at any given time. This is accomplished by creating a menu that displays all the possible options.

This chapter describes how to create a menu. The entry routine is converted to a subroutine, and a function is added that allows corrections to be made to the data after all the information has been entered.

Displaying Program Functions

The options available to the Operator should be displayed first.

```
Step 1.   Type In and Press Enter:

        800 CLS: REM  Alternate:  800 PRINT CHR$(12);
        810 PRINT TAB(D1 +11);"PAYROLL FUNCTIONS"
        820 PRINT TAB(D1 +11);"________________"
        830 PRINT TAB(D1 +6);"1) DISPLAY EMPLOYEE RECORDS"
        840 PRINT TAB(D1 +6);"2) DISPLAY TOTAL HOURS & PAY"
        850 PRINT TAB(D1 +6);"3) CORRECT HOURS"
        860 PRINT TAB(D1 +6);"4) DISPLAY PAY & DEDUCTIONS"
        870 PRINT TAB(D1 +6);"5) PRINT PAY CHECKS"
        880 PRINT TAB(D1 +6);"6) PRINT PAYROLL SUMMARY"
        900 PRINT TAB(D1 +6);"8) STORE PAYROLL"
        910 PRINT TAB(D1 +6);"9) RETRIEVE PAYROLL"
```

Line 800 clears the Video Screen.

Lines 810 and 820 display a heading for the menu.

Lines 830 to 910 display the options the Operator may select for the Payroll Program.

Selecting the Function to be Used

An Input routine must be included to accept the option the Operator selects.

```
Step 2.   Type In and Press Enter:

        940 PRINT:PRINT TAB(D1 +11);"SELECT FUNCTION";
        950 A = 0:INPUT A
        970 ON A GOSUB 2500,2000,3000,2200,5000,6000,7000,8000,9000
        980 GOTO 800
        2200 RETURN
        3000 RETURN
        5000 RETURN
        6000 RETURN
        7000 RETURN
        8000 RETURN
        9000 RETURN
```

Line 940 displays the prompt to the Operator indicating an option may be selected.

Line 950 is the INPUT Instruction.

Line 970 is an ON GOSUB Instruction which uses the value of the Variable A to count over to the appropriate Line Number to which the program is to proceed. This works the same way as the ON GOTO Instruction, except the GOSUB Instruction returns control of the program to Line 980 when a RETURN Instruction is encountered in the subroutine.

Line 980 directs the program back up to the beginning of the menu display so another function may be selected.

Lines 2200 to 9000 have not been assigned functions at this time. A RETURN Instruction is temporarily assigned to each line to prevent an error message from occurring if the Operator selects one of these options before the function is added to the program.

Ending the Program

After the program has run through all of the appropriate functions, the Operator can terminate its operation.

```
Step 3.  Type In and Press Enter:

       930 PRINT TAB(D1+5);"11) END THE PROGRAM"
       960 IF A=11 THEN GOTO 990
       990 PRINT:PRINT "THE END":END
       RUN
```

Line 930 adds the option to end the program to the menu of functions.

Line 960 occurs after the INPUT Instruction and before the ON GOSUB Instruction to determine when the option to end the program has been selected.

Line 990 displays the message "The End" and terminates the program's operation with an END Instruction.

```
Step 4.  The Computer Displays:

                        PAYROLL FUNCTIONS
                        ------------------
             1) DISPLAY EMPLOYEE RECORDS
             2) DISPLAY TOTAL HOURS & PAY
             3) CORRECT HOURS
             4) DISPLAY PAY & DEDUCTIONS
             5) PRINT PAY CHECKS
             6) PRINT PAYROLL SUMMARY
             8) STORE PAYROLL
             9) RETRIEVE PAYROLL
            10) DISPLAY EMPLOYEE RECORDS
            11) END THE PROGRAM

                        SELECT FUNCTION? _
```

Converting Functions to Subroutines

In order to test the program as it was being developed, the entry routine was not written as a subroutine. This function now needs to be converted to a subroutine.

Step 5. Type In and Press Enter:

```
700 GOSUB 1000:REM  Enter Employee Hours
1410 RETURN
```

Line 700 directs the program to the entry routine before the program reaches the menu because information must be entered before the other routines in the program can be used.

Line 1410 converts the entry routine to a subroutine.

Corrections after Entry

The correction subroutine is currently written to correct information immediately after it is entered for each employee. It can now be expanded so that corrections can be made after the information for all the employees has been entered. In order to do this, the program must display the hours and allow the Operator to select the employee to be changed. A standard display routine is used to indicate the hours.

Step 6. Type In and Press Enter:

```
3000 D=0:RESTORE
3010 FOR N=1 TO W
3020 IF D>0 THEN GOTO 3070
3030 CLS: REM  Alternate:  3030 PRINT CHR$(12);
3040 D=3:PRINT TAB(D1+13);"CORRECT HOURS":PRINT
3050 PRINT " #";TAB(5);"NAME";
3060 PRINT TAB(17);"HOURS FOR WEEK 1  WEEK 2"
3070 GOSUB 9500:REM  Retrieve Employee Information
3080 IF C<1 THEN GOTO 3120
3090 PRINT E;TAB(5);N$;TAB(28);W1(E);TAB(36);W2(E)
3100 D=D+1:IF D<D3 OR N=W THEN GOTO 3120
3110 GOSUB 3150:D=0:IF N=0 THEN GOTO 3000
3120 NEXT N
3130 GOSUB 3150:D=0:IF N=0 THEN GOTO 3000
3140 RETURN
3150 PRINT:PRINT TAB(D1+7);"TO CONTINUE PRESS (ENTER)"
3160 PRINT TAB(D1+11);"CORRECT EMPLOYEE #";
3170 A$="":INPUT A$:A=VAL(A$):IF A>0 THEN GOTO 3200
3180 RETURN
RUN
```

Lines 3000 to 3120 form the same kind of display routine used to display the workers' Gross Pay and the employee records.

Lines 3130 and 3140 occur at the end of the display routine. They direct the program to Line 3150 to determine if a change is to be made to one of the employee's hours. If a change is to be made, the value in the Variable N is set to zero by the correction subroutine. When this happens, the program is directed to the beginning of the employee display, IF N=0 THEN GOTO 3000.

Lines 3160 and 3170 add the option to change an employee's hours by entering a number. If no number is entered, the pause control returns the program to the originating GOSUB Instruction. If an employee number is entered, the program progresses to Line 3200.

Line 3170 uses the VAL Instruction to convert the String response in the INPUT Instruction, A$, into a numeric value, A.

Testing the Display

Run the program now to test the display routine. When the hours for Harrison are requested, enter 43 hours for week one and 35 hours for week two. When the hours for Samuels are requested, enter 41 hours for week one and 44 hours for week two. When the hours for Johnson are requested, enter 28 hours for week one and 35 hours for week two. The following display will appear.

```
Step 7.  The Computer Displays:

                         CORRECT HOURS

    #  NAME      HOURS FOR WEEK 1  WEEK 2
    1  Harrison              43       35
    2  Samuels               41       44
    3  Johnson               28       35

            TO CONTINUE PRESS (ENTER)
            CORRECT EMPLOYEE #? _
```

Retrieving Employee Data

Once the employee number has been selected, the information from the employee's records must be retrieved. When the record to be processed is located, the program proceeds to the subroutine that allows individual hours to be changed.

Step 8. Type In and Press Enter:

```
3200 RESTORE
3210 FOR N = 1 TO W
3220 GOSUB 9500:REM  Retrieve Employee Information
3225 IF C <1 THEN GOTO 3240
3230 IF E = A THEN GOTO 3250
3240 NEXT N:N = 0:RETURN
3250 GOSUB 3500:GOSUB 4000:REM  Payroll Calculations
3260 N = 0:RETURN
```

A   Operator's Response (Employee # to Change)
E   Employee Number

Lines 3210 to 3240 form a **FOR NEXT** Loop that goes through all of the employee record files until the correct employee number appears. When this happens, E=A, Line 3230 directs the program to Line 3250.

If the employee's number is not discovered in the records, Line 3240 sets the value of the Variable N to zero and returns the program to the originating GOSUB Instruction. When the value of the Variable N is zero, the program returns to the beginning of the display routine for the corrections.

Line 3250 directs the program to the correction routine, GOSUB 3500, then to the routine that calculates the Gross Pay, GOSUB 4000.

Line 3260 sets the value of the Variable N to zero and returns the program to the initiating GOSUB Instruction.

Initial Program Information

When the program is first started, the initial lines can be used to establish basic information about the Pay Period to be processed, including the current date, the ending date of the Pay Period, and a number for the Pay Period.

Step 9.   Type In and Press Enter:

```
510 PRINT TAB(D1 +12);"PAYROLL PROGRAM"
520 PRINT TAB(D1 +12);"----------------"
530 PRINT TAB(D1);"ENTER DATE MM – DD – YY (Jan 10: 01 – 10 – 84)"
540 PRINT "TODAY'S DATE";:INPUT TD$
550 PRINT "ENDING DATE FOR PAY PERIOD";:INPUT ED$
560 PRINT "ENTER # FOR THIS PAY PERIOD";:INPUT PP$
```

Lines 510 and 520 provide a heading for the program.

Lines 530 to 550 determine the dates that will be required to record the information for the current Pay Period.

Line 560 specifies a number for the current Pay Period. This number will be used by the storage and retrieval routines.

Disk and Cassette Storage

More often than not, the information created by a program will be needed at a later date. This chapter shows how to store this information on either Disks or Cassette Tapes. Once recorded, it can be retrieved whenever, and as often, as necessary.

Pages 45 to 49 showed how program lines with the names of Variables are recorded. While this procedure records the names, it does not store any of the information in the Variables. This chapter shows how information from a program is transferred from the Variables to a Disk or Cassette Tape. This procedure does not store the names of the Variables with the information, so information created by one program can be used by other programs in an unlimited number of ways.

INFORMATION STORAGE

The following steps summarize the actions a storage routine must take.

1. A prompt is displayed to alert the Operator that information is about to be stored. This allows the Operator to make sure that the equipment is physically ready.

2. After the Operator indicates that the Disk or Cassette Tape is ready, the program must initialize communication with the storage device using an OPEN Instruction.

3. Information that identifies the file is recorded first.

4. Individual items are then recorded.

5. After all the information is recorded, the communication channel to the Disk Drive or Cassette Tape Recorder is closed.

The specific instructions used to perform these functions are described below.

Storing Information

Before information can be stored, a communication channel to the storage device must be opened. The data is then recorded using a variation of the PRINT Instruction. After the information has been stored, the communication channel to the storage device is closed.

Step 1. Type In and Press Enter:
8040 A$ = "PAY" + PP$
8050 OPEN"O",1,A$
8060 PRINT#1,ED$
8070 PRINT#1,W
8090 PRINT#1,W1(N),W2(N),GP(N)
8140 CLOSE#1

ED$	Ending Date of Pay Period
PP$	Pay Period Number
W	Number of Employees
W1( )	Number of hours for week one
W2( )	Number of Hours for week two
GP ( )	Gross Pay

Line 8040 creates a file name for the information to be stored by combining the word "PAY" with the number of the Pay Period stored in the Variable PP$, see Line 560 on page 83.

Line 8050 contains the OPEN Instruction which opens a communication channel to the storage device. The "O" in the instruction indicates that the OPEN Instruction is for "Output."

Lines 8060 to 8090 transfer the information stored in the Variables and Arrays from the computer's memory to the storage device.

Line 8140 uses the CLOSE Instruction to close the communication channel to the storage device.

The program lines indicated above are used to store information on Disk. These instructions must be modified for Cassette Tape storage.

Step 1. IBM PC Cassette. Type In and Press Enter:
8040 A$ = "CAS1:PAY" + PP$

The Cassette Tape version adds the designation "CAS1:" to the file name to indicate the information is to be stored on the first Cassette Tape Recorder.

Processing All the Records

The Print Instruction in Line 8090 stores information for only one employee. A FOR NEXT Loop is used to process all of the employees.

```
Step 2.   Type In and Press Enter:

     8080 FOR N = 1 TO W
     8130 NEXT N
```

Lines 8080 and 8130 form a FOR NEXT Loop similar to the ones used in the display and entry routines.

Prompting the Operator

The Operator must be prompted to prepare the storage device before the program proceeds to the working part of the storage routine.

```
Step 3.   Type In and Press Enter:

     8000 CLS: REM  Alternate  8000 PRINT CHR$(12);
     8010 PRINT TAB(D1 + 8);"PREPARE TO STORE PAYROLL":PRINT
     8020 PRINT TAB(D1 + 4);"IS THE DISK READY (<Y> OR N)";
     8030 A$ = "":INPUT A$:IF A$ = "N" OR A$ = "n" THEN RETURN
```

Line 8000 clears the display.

Line 8010 indicates the function the program is waiting to perform.

Lines 8020 and 8030 halt the operation of the program until the Operator responds. This prompt also gives the Operator the option of discontinuing the storage function with a negative response to the question. If the No answer is selected, the program returns to the menu.

```
Step 3.   Cassette Tape.   Type In and Press Enter:

     8020 PRINT TAB(D1 + 2);"IS THE RECORDER READY (<Y> OR N)";
```

Ending the Storage Function

The program initially proceeds to the storage function with a GOSUB Instruction. A RETURN Instruction must be used to terminate this function and return the program to the menu of functions.

```
Step 4.   Type In and Press Enter:

     8280 RETURN
     RUN
```

INFORMATION RETRIEVAL

The retrieval routine must follow the same sequence of operations as the storage routine so that the information will be assigned to the appropriate Variables and Arrays.

Retrieving Information

To retrieve information from the storage device, a communication channel to the storage device must be opened. A variation of the INPUT Instruction then transfers the information from the Disk or Cassette Tape to the Arrays and Variables in the computer's memory.

Step 5. Type In and Press Enter:

```
9040 A$ = "PAY" + PP$
9050 OPEN "I",1,A$
9060 INPUT#1,ED$
9070 INPUT#1,W
9090 INPUT#1,W1(N),W2(N),GP(N)
9140 CLOSE#1
```

Line 9040 creates a name for the file using the word "PAY" and the number of the Pay Period stored in the Variable PP$.

Line 9050 opens the communication channel to the storage device. The "I" in the instruction indicates that the OPEN Instruction is for "Input."

Lines 9060 to 9090 use a variation of the INPUT Instruction to transfer the information from the storage device to the Variables and Arrays in the computer's memory.

Line 9140 closes the communication channel.

Step 5. IBM PC Cassette. Type In and Press Enter:

```
9040 A$ = "CAS1:PAY" + PP$
```

The file name for the IBM PC is expanded to include the "CAS1:" designation to indicate the copy is being retrieved from the first Cassette Tape Recorder.

Processing All the Employees

Line 9090 retrieves the information for only one employee. A FOR NEXT Loop must be used to retrieve the information for all of the employees.

```
Step 6.  Type In and Press Enter:

     9080 FOR N = 1 TO W
     9130 NEXT N
```

This type of FOR NEXT Loop has already been used on several routines.

Prompting the Operator

The Operator must be alerted to prepare the storage device before the information is retrieved.

```
Step 7.  Type In and Press Enter:

     9000 CLS: REM  Alternate:  9000 PRINT CHR$(12);
     9010 PRINT TAB(D1 + 6);"PREPARE TO RETRIEVE PAYROLL":PRINT
     9020 PRINT TAB(D1 + 4);"IS THE DISK READY ( <Y> OR N)";
     9030 A$ = "":INPUT A$:IF A$ = "N" OR A$ = "n" THEN RETURN
```

Line 9000 clears the display.

Line 9010 describes the function the computer is about to perform.

Lines 9020 and 9030 stop the program and wait for the Operator's response. A "No" response terminates the routine with a RETURN Instruction.

```
Step 7.  Cassette Tape.  Type In and Press Enter:

     9020 PRINT TAB(D1 + 2);"IS THE RECORDER READY ( <Y> OR N)";
```

Terminating the Retrieval Routine

The program initially selects this retrieval routine using a GOSUB Instruction. A RETURN Instruction must be added to terminate the routine.

```
Step 8.  Type In and Press Enter:

     9150 RETURN
     RUN
```

The retrieval routine may be tested by recovering the information that was stored when the storage function was tested.

RECORDING THE PAY PERIOD NUMBER ON DISK

The Pay Period number serves an important function for Disk-based systems. It is used as part of the file name that records the data for the current Pay Period. If the number used is the same as a file that already exists, the existing file will be erased and replaced by the new file.

To eliminate the possibility of an error, the Pay Period number for the current record can be stored as a separate file immediately after the information is recorded. The next time the program is run, the Pay Period number is retrieved from this file and incremented by a value of one. Using a stored file in this manner eliminates any chance of an Operator accidentally assigning the wrong number to the Pay Period to be processed.

Storing the Pay Period Number

A short routine is used to store the number of the current Pay Period using a file name "LastPay."

Step 9. Type In and Press Enter:

```
8250 OPEN "O",1,"LASTPAY"
8260 PRINT#1,PP$
8270 CLOSE#1
```

Retrieving the Pay Period

A similar sequence of instructions must be used to retrieve the number of the last Pay Period from the Disk.

Step 10. Type In and Press Enter:

```
9250 OPEN "I",1,"LASTPAY"
9260 INPUT#1,PP$
9270 CLOSE#1
```

Prompting the Operator

The retrieval of the Pay Period number comes after the ending date for the current Pay Period is entered and before the hours are entered. The Operator must therefore be alerted to make sure that the Disk Drive is ready.

Step 11. Type In and Press Enter:

```
560 GOSUB 9200:IF PP$ = "" THEN GOTO 560
9200 CLS: REM  Alternate:  9200 PRINT CHR$(12);
9210 PRINT TAB(D1 + 4);"PREPARE TO RETRIEVE PAY PERIOD #"
9220 PRINT TAB(D1 + 4);"IS THE DISK READY ( <Y> OR N)";
9230 A$ = "":INPUT A$:IF A$ = "N" OR A$ = "n" THEN RETURN
9280 RETURN
```

Line 560 directs the program to the subroutine that retrieves the Pay Period number.
Lines 9200 and 9210 alert the Operator to the action that must be performed.
Lines 9220 and 9230 are the prompt that stops the program until the Operator responds.
Line 9280 terminates the subroutine.

Changing the Pay Period Number

The number of the Pay Period must be incremented by a value of one. To do this, the String stored in the Variable PP$ must first be converted to a numeric value. This value is then incremented by a value of one. The new value must then be reconverted to a String for use at a later time as a part of the file name.

Step 12. Type In and Press Enter:

```
570 A = VAL(PP$) + 1:PP$ = STR$(A)
575 L = LEN(PP$) – 1:PP$ = RIGHT$(PP$,L)
```

Line 570 converts the value of the Variable PP$ to a number and adds a value of one. It then reconverts this new value into a String.
Line 575 removes the space from the left side of the String.

Advanced Calculations

So far, the program has only performed the simplest calculations with the employee hours. This chapter will add the more detailed calculations required to determine payroll deductions.

Depending on personal needs and interests, the information in this section can be used in several ways. If the Payroll Program is not going to be used, read this section for a general understanding of how to translate instructions for manual calculations into program lines. For a better understanding of the principles, enter the calculations that do not require a lot of data. To see the full power of the computer or to create a functioning payroll program, type in all of the information provided.

The calculations described in this section include: overtime, Federal Income Tax withholding, Social Security withholding, California State Income Tax withholding, California State Disability Insurance, and Net Pay. Instructions for performing the calculations are supplied by the appropriate government agencies in booklets called "Employer's Tax Guides." The results of each calculation are stored in a special Array. The names of the calculations and the Arrays are listed in the table below. Abbreviations for the names of some of the calculations are also indicated.

```
                      PAYROLL CALCULATIONS

Name                          Abbreviation              Array
Federal Income Tax                 FIT                  FT(E)
Social Security Tax                FICA                 SS(E)
State Income Tax                   SIT                  ST(E)
State Disability Ins.              SDI                  SD(E)
Gross Pay                                               GP(E)
Regular Earnings                                        RE(E)
Overtime Earnings                                       OE(E)
Net Pay                                                 NP(E)
```

DISPLAYING DEDUCTIONS

The Gross Pay and deductions must be displayed to verify that the correct amounts are being processed. There will be several columns on this display, so two variations are shown. The first version displays the copy for computers using an 80-column screen on which the information for each employee occupies a single line of the display. The second version shows the routine for computers using 40-column screens. This variation divides the information for each employee into two lines of the display.

Step 1.   Type In and Press Enter:

```
2200 D = 0:RESTORE
2205 T = 0
2210 FOR N = 1 TO W
2220 IF D > 0 THEN GOTO 2280
2230 CLS: REM  Alternate:  2230 PRINT CHR$(12);
2240 D = 3:PRINT TAB(D1 + 12);"CURRENT PAYROLL":PRINT
2250 PRINT " #";TAB(5);"NAME";TAB(17);"GROSS PAY";
2260 PRINT TAB(30);"FITA";TAB(38);"FICA";
2270 PRINT TAB(46);"SIT";TAB(54);"SDI"
2280 GOSUB 9500:REM  Retrieve Employee Information
2290 IF C < 1 THEN GOTO 2350
2300 PRINT E;TAB(5);N$;TAB(17);GP(E);TAB(30);FT(E);
2310 PRINT TAB(38);SS(E);TAB(46);ST(E);TAB(54);SD(E)
2325 T = T + GP(E)
2330 D = D + 1:IF D < D3 OR N = W THEN GOTO 2350
2340 GOSUB 2360:D = 0
2350 NEXT N
2355 PRINT:PRINT "THE TOTAL PAYROLL IS $";T
2360 PRINT:PRINT TAB(D1 + 7);"TO CONTINUE PRESS (ENTER)";
2370 INPUT A$:RETURN
RUN
```

Lines 2205, 2325, and 2355 calculate and display the total payroll. The rest of the lines form a standard display routine.

The following lines must be changed to allow this display to work with computers using 40-column screens.

```
Step 1.   40 Column Conversion.   Type In and Press Enter:

        2240 D = 4:PRINT TAB(D1 +12);"CURRENT PAYROLL":PRINT
        2250 PRINT " #";TAB(5);"NAME";TAB(15);"GROSS PAY";
        2260 PRINT TAB(30);"FITA":PRINT TAB(16);"FICA";
        2270 PRINT TAB(24);"SIT";TAB(32);"SDI":PRINT
        2300 PRINT E;TAB(5);N$;TAB(15);GP(E);TAB(30);FT(E)
        2310 PRINT TAB(16);SS(E);TAB(24);ST(E);TAB(32);SD(E)
        2320 PRINT
        2330 D = D + 3:IF  D <D3 OR N = W THEN GOTO 2350
        RUN
```

Line 2240 increases the value of the Variable D to a value of four because an additional line of the display is used for the headings of the columns.

Line 2260 uses two PRINT Instructions to break the display with FITA on one line and FICA on a second line.

Line 2300 is changed to drop the semicolon at the end of the line so that information from Line 2300 appears on one line of the display and information from Line 2310 appears on a second.

Line 2310 changes the TAB Instructions for the 40-column display.

Line 2320 is added to create a blank line after the data for each employee is displayed.

Line 2330 is changed to indicate that information about each employee requires three lines of the display, D=D+3.

Another variation of the display uses an instruction called PRINT USING which displays information in specified formats. The conversions for this instruction are indicated below for computers with 80-column displays.

```
Step 1.   Alternate.  Type In and Press Enter:

      2300 PRINT E;TAB(5);N$;TAB(18);
      2302 PRINT USING "#####.##";GP(E);
      2304 PRINT USING "#####.##";FT(E);
      2306 PRINT USING "#####.##";SS(E);
      2308 PRINT USING "#####.##";ST(E);
      2310 PRINT USING "#####.##";SD(E)
      2355 PRINT:PRINT "THE TOTAL PAYROLL IS";
      2357 PRINT USING "$$#####.##";T
      RUN
```

In Lines 2302 to 2310, the PRINT USING Instruction is followed by a String representation of how the information is to be displayed. The "#" signs act as place holders. If there is no numeric digit for the "#" sign to the left of the decimal point, a space is displayed. This is somewhat similar to the TAB Instruction, except that the decimal points in the column will always be aligned. The "#" sign to the right of the decimal is displayed as zero if there is no other numeric digit. For example, if the PRINT USING Instruction is not used, the value of $1.50 is displayed as 1.5. But if the PRINT USING Instruction with "##.##" is used, the value will be displayed as 1.50. On the other hand, only the number of digits specified to the right of the decimal will be displayed. A value of 1.553 is displayed by the PRINT USING Instruction as 1.55.

In Line 2357, another variation of the PRINT USING format is used which includes the double dollar signs. The double dollar signs tell the computer to display the number preceded by a dollar sign. For example, when the value 1.5 is displayed with PRINT USING "$$##.##", the result is $1.50.

OVERTIME CALCULATIONS

Overtime must be calculated first because it changes the Gross Pay on which all other calculations are based. The calculation determines which week an employee has worked over 40 hours. For these weeks, the employee is paid time and a half for the hours in excess of 40.

```
        Step 2.  Type In and Press Enter:

4010 RT(E)=0:RE(E)=0:OT(E)=0:OE(E)=0
4020 FT(E)=0:SS(E)=0:ST(E)=0:SD(E)=0
4030 REM   Calculate Overtime
4040 IF W1(E)>40 THEN GOTO 4050
4045 RT(E)=W1(E):RE(E)=W1(E)*P:GOTO 4060
4050 RT(E)=40:OT(E)=W1(E)-40
4055 RE(E)=40*P:OE(E)=(W1(E)-40)*(P+P/2)
4060 IF W2(E)>40 THEN GOTO 4070
4065 RT(E)=RT(E)+W2(E):RE(E)=RE(E)+W2(E)*P:GOTO 4080
4070 RT(E)=RT(E)+40:OT(E)=OT(E)+W2(E)-40
4075 RE(E)=RE(E)+40*P:OE(E)=OE(E)+(W2(E)-40)*(P+P/2)
4080 RE(E)=INT(100*RE(E)+.5)/100
4085 OE(E)=INT(100*OE(E)+.5)/100
4090 GP(E)=RE(E)+OE(E)
```

Line 4010 clears all of the Variables of the Arrays for the current employee, E.

Line 4040 determines if the employee has worked over 40 hours. If he or she has, the program progresses to Line 4050. If the employee has worked 40 hours or less, the program drops to Line 4045.

Line 4045 records the regular hours and calculates the regular earnings by multiplying the number of hours worked by the rate of pay, W1(E)*P. The program then proceeds to week two, GOTO 4060.

Line 4040 records the first 40 hours worked in the Array RT( ). Regular earnings are then calculated for the first 40 hours, RE(E)=40*P. Overtime earnings are calculated by multiplying the time in excess of 40 hours, W1(E)-40, by a rate of pay equal to time and a half, P+P/2.

Line 4065 records the regular hours and calculates the regular earnings when 40 hours or less have been worked during week two. The main difference between Lines 4060 and 4065 is that Line 4065 adds the results of the calculation to any regular hours and earnings recorded for week one, RE(E)=RE(E)+W2(E)*P.

Lines 4070 and 4075 calculate the regular and overtime earnings for week two. The earnings from week two are added to any earnings recorded in week one.

Lines 4080 and 4085 round off the earnings to the nearest cent. The sequence of this calculation for Regular Earnings is indicated below.

1. The Regular Earnings are multiplied by 100. For example, 1.556 becomes 155.6 and 1.554 becomes 155.4.

2. A value of .5 is added to this amount. This extra amount increases any value equal to or greater than half a cent to the next penny. Thus, 155.6 becomes 156.1 and 155.4 becomes 155.9.

3. The INT Instruction drops off any value to the right of the decimal point. The value 156.1 becomes 156 and 155.9 becomes 155.

4. This value is then divided by 100. The value 156 becomes 1.56 and 155 becomes 1.55.

Line 4090 combines Regular Earnings with Overtime Earnings to establish the Gross Pay.

SOCIAL SECURITY TAX

Social Security Tax is a straight percentage of the Gross Pay, so it is fairly easy to calculate. The only complication is that when the cumulative Gross Pay for the year exceeds a certain amount, the tax is no longer charged.

For 1984 the Social Security withholding tax is 6.7 percent and the maximum taxable income is $37,800. The following addition to the program calculates the FICA deduction.

Step 3. Type In and Press Enter:

```
4100 REM  Social Security Tax  (FICA)
4110 PRINT:PRINT "HAS ";N$;" EARNED OVER $37,800 (Y/ <N>)";
4120 A$ = "":INPUT A$:A = 2:IF A$ = "Y" OR A$ = "y" THEN A = 1
4130 IF A = 1 THEN GOTO 4200
4140 SS(E) = GP(E) * 6.7/100:SS(E) = INT(100 * SS(E) + .5)/100
RUN
```

GP( )   Gross Pay
SS( )   FICA Withholding

Lines 4110 and 4130 ask the Operator if the current employee, N$, has earned over the specified amount. If an employee's pay scale makes it unlikely that this amount will be reached, these three lines can be left off.

Line 4140 calculates the FICA Withholding by multiplying the employee's Gross Pay by the prescribed percentage, 6.7/100. This value is then rounded to the nearest cent.

CALIFORNIA STATE DISABILITY INSURANCE

All employees pay California State Disability Insurance. Originally, this deduction was calculated as a straight percentage of wages with no ceiling. Now the deduction is calculated the same way as FICA withholding. The rate is .9 percent of the first $21,900.

Step 4. Type In and Press Enter:

```
4150 REM  California State Disability Insurance
4160 PRINT "HAS ";N$;" EARNED OVER $21,900 (Y/ <N>)";
4170 A$ = "":INPUT A$:A = 2:IF A$ = "Y" OR A$ = "y" THEN A = 1
4180 SD(E) = 0:IF A = 1 THEN GOTO 4200
4190 SD(E) = GP(E) * .9/100:SD(E) = INT(100 * SD(E) + .5)/100
RUN
```

This sequence of steps is the same as the calculations for FICA withholding. Only the percentage and limit differ. The Array SD(E) records the result of the calculation.

FEDERAL INCOME TAX

Computerizing Federal Income Tax deductions is not as complicated as one might expect. This is because the instructions for calculating the withholding deductions are written in a very precise sequence of steps. This is exactly the way the computer processes information. It is therefore only necessary to translate these steps into instructions the computer can follow. Shown below is an extract from page 19 of the 1984 Federal Employer's Tax Guide, Circular E.

Income Tax Withholding— Percentage Method

(If you use the wage bracket tables on pages 22 through 41, you may skip this section.)

If you do not want to use the wage bracket tables to figure how much income tax to withhold, you can use a percentage computation based on the table below and the appropriate rate table. This method works for any number of withholding allowances the employee claims.

Percentage Method Income Tax Withholding Table

Payroll Period	One withholding allowance
Weekly	$19.23
Biweekly	38.46
Semimonthly	41.66
Monthly	83.33
Quarterly	250.00
Semiannually	500.00
Annually	1,000.00
Daily or miscellaneous (each day of the payroll period) .	3.85

Use these steps to figure the income tax to withhold under the percentage method:

(a) Multiply one withholding allowance (see table above) by the number of allowances the employee claims.

(b) Subtract that amount from the employee's wages.

(c) Determine amount to withhold from appropriate table on pages 20 and 21.

Example.—An unmarried employee is paid $150 weekly. This employee has in effect a Form W–4 claiming one personal allowance and the special withholding allowance. Using the percentage method, figure the income tax as follows:

(1) Total wage payment............... $150.00

(2) One allowance........... $19.23

The instructions list three steps in preparing the income tax to be withheld.

a. The withholding allowance from the table is multiplied by the number of exemptions the employee claims. The withholding allowance for the biweekly pay period is $38.46 and the number of exemptions is stored by the program in the Variable X. This step can therefore be translated into: 38.46 * X.

b. The withholding allowance is subtracted from the employee's Gross Pay. The employee's Gross Pay is recorded in the Array GP( ).

c. The withholding amount is then determined from the Tax Tables.

The following steps demonstrate how these calculations are performed.

FIT Withholding Allowance

The calculations from Steps a. and b. above can be incorporated into one formula. The results of the calculations are stored in the Variable F which becomes the taxable federal income.

<table>
<tr><td colspan="2">Percentage Method Income Tax Withholding Table</td><td rowspan="2">Use these steps to figure the income tax to withhold under the percentage method:
(a) Multiply one withholding allowance (see table above) by the number of allowances the employee claims.
(b) Subtract that amount from the employee's wages.
(c) Determine amount to withhold from appropriate table on pages 20 and 21.</td></tr>
<tr><td>Payroll Period</td><td>One withholding allowance</td></tr>
<tr><td>Weekly . . . .</td><td>$19.23</td><td></td></tr>
<tr><td>Biweekly . . . .</td><td>38.46</td><td></td></tr>
<tr><td>Semimonthly . . . . .</td><td>41.66</td><td></td></tr>
<tr><td>Monthly . . . .</td><td>83.33</td><td></td></tr>
<tr><td>Quarterly . . . . . .</td><td>250.00</td><td></td></tr>
<tr><td>Semiannually . . . . .</td><td>500.00</td><td></td></tr>
<tr><td>Annually . . . .</td><td>1,000.00</td><td></td></tr>
<tr><td>Daily or miscellaneous (each day of the payroll period) .</td><td>3.85</td><td></td></tr>
</table>

Step 5. Type In and Press Enter:

```
4200 REM  Federal Income Tax  (FIT)
4210 F = GP(E) - 38.46 * X
```

F   Taxable Income
GP( )   Gross Pay
X   Number of Exemptions

Line 4210 multiplies the biweekly withholding allowance by the number of exemptions and subtracts this from the Gross Pay to determine the taxable income.

Selecting the Tax Table

The Tax Tables used to calculate withholding vary according to the pay schedule and whether or not the employee is married. Table 2 is used to determine the taxes for a biweekly pay schedule. The selection of the section of the table to be used is determined by the Marital Status for the employee as recorded in the Variable M. For this Variable, a value of one is used for single taxpayers, two for married, and three for head of household.

Step 6. Type In and Press Enter:

```
4220 ON M GOTO 4230,4240,4230
4230 REM  Tax Table 2a for Single Person and Head of House
4240 REM  Tax Table 2b for Married Person
```

Line 4220 uses the value in the Variable M to select the appropriate table.

Table 2a for Single Taxpayers

The Tax Tables can be almost directly translated into computer language. For example, the instruction from the first line of the table reads "If the amount of the wages is not over $54, the amount of the tax is zero." In computer language this becomes IF F=<54 THEN FT(E)=0. The Variable F is the taxable wages and the Array FT( ) holds the federal tax deduction. The translation for the remainder of the table is indicated below.

TABLE 2—If the Payroll Period With Respect to an Employee is Biweekly

(a) SINGLE person—including head of household:

If the amount of wages is:		The amount of income tax to be withheld shall be:	of excess over—
Not over $54		0	
Over—	But not over—		
$54	—$158	12%	—$54
$158	—$365	$12.48 plus 15%	—$158
$365	—$554	$43.53 plus 19%	—$365
$554	—$846	$79.44 plus 25%	—$554
$846	—$1,069	$152.44 plus 30%	—$846
$1,069	—$1,273	$219.34 plus 34%	—$1,069
$1,273		$288.70 plus 37%	—$1,273

(b) MARRIED person—

If the amount of wages is:		The amount of income tax to be withheld shall be:	of excess over—
Not over $92		0	
Over—	But not over—		
$92	—$369	12%	—$92
$369	—$738	$33.24 plus 17%	—$369
$738	—$908	$95.97 plus 22%	—$738
$908	—$1,112	$133.37 plus 25%	—$908
$1,112	—$1,315	$184.37 plus 28%	—$1,112
$1,315	—$1,723	$241.21 plus 33%	—$1,315
$1,723		$375.85 plus 37%	—$1,723

Step 7. Type In and Press Enter:

```
4231 IF F = <54 THEN GOTO 4250
4232 IF F = <158 THEN FT(E) = 12/100 * (F − 54):GOTO 4250
4233 IF F = <365 THEN FT(E) = 12.48 + 15/100 * (F − 158):GOTO 4250
4234 IF F = <554 THEN FT(E) = 43.53 + 19/100 * (F − 365):GOTO 4250
4235 IF F = <846 THEN FT(E) = 79.44 + 25/100 * (F − 554):GOTO 4250
4236 IF F = <1069 THEN FT(E) = 152.44 + 30/100 * (F − 846):GOTO 4250
4237 IF F = <1273 THEN FT(E) = 219.34 + 34/100 * (F − 1069):GOTO 4250
4238 FT(E) = 288.7 + 37/100 * (F − 1273):GOTO 4250
```

To see how the program would process the information, assume the employee has taxable wages of $250.

1. The value of the Variable F is greater than 54 so the program drops from Line 4231 to 4232.

2. The value of the Variable F is greater than 158 so the program drops to Line 4233.

3. The value of the Variable F is less than 365 so the instructions to the right of the THEN Instruction are processed.

4. A value of 12.48 is added to 15 percent (15/100) of the taxable wages in excess of 158, F − 158.

5. The program progresses to Line 4250.

Table 2b for Married Taxpayers

The Tax Table for married taxpayers is identical in structure to the table for single people. Only the values differ.

TABLE 2—If the Payroll Period With Respect to an Employee is Biweekly

(a) SINGLE person—including head of household:

If the amount of wages is:		The amount of income tax to be withheld shall be:	
Not over $54 0			
Over—	**But not over—**		**of excess over—**
$54	—$158 ....12%		—$54
$158	—$365 ....$12.48 plus 15%		—$158
$365	—$554 ....$43.53 plus 19%		—$365
$554	—$846 ....$79.44 plus 25%		—$554
$846	—$1,069...$152.44 plus 30%		—$846
$1,069	—$1,273...$219.34 plus 34%		—$1,069
$1,273	...........$288.70 plus 37%		—$1,273

(b) MARRIED person—

If the amount of wages is:		The amount of income tax to be withheld shall be:	
Not over $92 0			
Over—	**But not over—**		**of excess over—**
$92	—$369 ....12%		—$92
$369	—$738 ....$33.24 plus 17%		—$369
$738	—$908 ....$95.97 plus 22%		—$738
$908	—$1,112...$133.37 plus 25%		—$908
$1,112	—$1,315...$184.37 plus 28%		—$1,112
$1,315	—$1,723...$241.21 plus 33%		—$1,315
$1,723	...........$375.85 plus 37%		—$1,723

Step 8. Type In and Press Enter:

```
4241 IF F = <92 THEN GOTO 4250
4242 IF F = <369 THEN FT(E) = 12/100 * (F − 92) : GOTO 4250
4243 IF F = <738 THEN FT(E) = 33.24 + 17/100 * (F − 369) : GOTO 4250
4244 IF F = <908 THEN FT(E) = 95.97 + 22/100 * (F − 738) : GOTO 4250
4245 IF F = <1112 THEN FT(E) = 133.37 + 25/100 * (F − 908) : GOTO 4250
4246 IF F = <1315 THEN FT(E) = 184.37 + 28/100 * (F − 1112) : GOTO 4250
4247 IF F = <1723 THEN FT(E) = 241.21 + 33/100 * (F − 1315) : GOTO 4250
4248 FT(E) = 375.85 + 37/100 * (F − 1723) : GOTO 4250
```

Completing the FIT Deduction

The FIT deduction needs to be rounded off to the nearest cent. The tax allowance may also have created a negative deduction that needs to be set to zero. For example, suppose an employee only works one day during a Pay Period and has four dependents. The wage might be $40, but the deduction allowance would be over $150, creating a negative tax. This value must be changed to zero.

Step 9. Type In and Press Enter:

```
4250 FT(E) = INT(100 * FT(E) + .5)/100
4255 IF FT(E) <0 THEN FT(E) = 0
RUN
```

Line 4250 rounds off the deduction to the nearest cent following the same sequence described on page 95.

Line 4255 determines if the value of FT(E) is less than zero and sets it to zero when this is the case.

CALIFORNIA STATE INCOME TAX

The California State Income Tax withholding calculations are more involved than the federal because there are three different tables with an optional fourth table. Fortunately, the Tax Tables are written in the same precise language as the federal. The steps for calculating the tax are reproduced below from the California Employer's Guide for 1984.

```
               CALIFORNIA WITHHOLDING SCHEDULES FOR 1984

               METHOD B - EXACT CALCULATION METHOD

THIS METHOD IS BASED UPON APPLYING A GIVEN PERCENTAGE TO THE WAGES (AFTER
DEDUCTIONS) WHICH FALL WITHIN A TAXABLE INCOME CLASS, ADDING TO THIS PRODUCT
THE ACCUMULATED TAX FOR ALL LOWER TAX BRACKETS, AND THEN SUBTRACTING A TAX
CREDIT BASED UPON THE NUMBER OF ALLOWANCES CLAIMED ON THE EMPLOYEE'S WITH-
HOLDING ALLOWANCE CERTIFICATE (CALIFORNIA FORM DE-4 OR FEDERAL FORM W-4).
THIS METHOD ALSO TAKES INTO CONSIDERATION THE SPECIAL TREATMENT OF ADDITIONAL
ALLOWANCES FOR ESTIMATED DEDUCTIONS.

THE STEPS IN COMPUTING THE AMOUNT OF TAX TO BE WITHHELD ARE AS FOLLOWS:

STEP (1)   IF THE EMPLOYEE CLAIMS ANY ADDITIONAL WITHHOLDING ALLOWANCES FOR
           ESTIMATED DEDUCTIONS, SUBTRACT THE AMOUNT SHOWN IN "TABLE A -
           ESTIMATED DEDUCTION TABLE" FROM THE GROSS SALARIES AND WAGES.

STEP (2)   SUBTRACT THE STANDARD DEDUCTION AMOUNT SHOWN IN "TABLE B - STANDARD
           DEDUCTION TABLE" TO ARRIVE AT THE EMPLOYEE'S TAXABLE INCOME.

STEP (3)   USE "TABLE D - TAX RATE TABLE" FOR THE PAYROLL PERIOD AND MARITAL
           STATUS TO FIND THE APPLICABLE LINE ON WHICH THE TAXABLE INCOME IS
           LOCATED.  PERFORM THE INDICATED CALCULATIONS TO ARRIVE AT THE
           COMPUTED TAX.

STEP (4)   SUBTRACT THE TAX CREDIT SHOWN IN "TABLE C - TAX CREDIT TABLE"* FROM
           THE COMPUTED TAX TO ARRIVE AT THE AMOUNT OF TAX TO BE WITHHELD.

       *   IF THE EMPLOYEE USES ADDITIONAL ALLOWANCES FOR ESTIMATED DEDUCTIONS,
           SUCH ALLOWANCES MUST NOT BE USED IN THE DETERMINATION OF TAX CREDITS
           TO BE SUBTRACTED.
```

Step 1 refers to an additional withholding allowance that can be used for state taxes but not for federal. This means that an additional Variable must be added to the employee records. For this reason, this step is described in Appendix A.

Step 2 refers to subtracting a standard deduction (derived from Table B) from the Gross Pay to determine the taxable wages. This table has four deductions based on Marital Status.

Step 3 uses Tax Tables similar to the federal tables to determine the amount of tax due. The main difference between these tables and the federal ones is that these have a separate table for Head of Household.

Step 4 introduces a table for a tax credit allowance. This table is based on Marital Status and the number of Tax Exemptions.

The following description evaluates each of these tables in detail.

California Standard Deduction

Table B divides taxpayers into four groups: single taxpayers, married taxpayers with less than two exemptions, married taxpayers with two or more allowances, and unmarried heads of households. This means that both the Variable M which records the Marital Status and the Variable X which records the number of Tax Exemptions must be used.

```
            CALIFORNIA WITHHOLDING SCHEDULES FOR 1984

            METHOD B---EXACT CALCULATION METHOD

            TABLE B - STANDARD DEDUCTION TABLE
```

PAYROLL PERIOD	SINGLE	MARRIED		UNMARRIED HEADS OF HOUSEHOLD
		ALLOWANCES ON DE-4 OR W-4.		
		"0" OR "1"	"2" OR MORE	
WEEKLY	29	29	58	58
BIWEEKLY	58	58	116	116
SEMI-MONTHLY	63	63	126	126
MONTHLY	126	126	252	252
QUARTERLY	378	378	755	755
SEMI-ANNUAL	755	755	1510	1510
ANNUAL	1510	1510	3020	3020
DAILY/MISCELLANEOUS	6	6	12	12

Step 10.   Type In and Press Enter:

```
4400 REM  State Income Tax
4410 ON M GOTO 4420,4430,4440
4420 S = GP(E) – 58:GOTO 4450
4430 IF X <2 THEN GOTO 4420
4440 S = GP(E) – 116
```

GP( )   Gross Pay
M   Marital Status
S   Taxable Income, State
X   Number of Exemptions

Line 4410 uses the Marital Status in the Variable M to select the deduction allowance.

Line 4420 subtracts the deduction for single taxpayers.

Line 4430 determines the deduction for married taxpayers. If fewer than two exemptions are declared, $X < 2$, the program is directed to the deduction for single taxpayers. Otherwise, the program drops to Line 4440.

Line 4440 determines the deduction for heads of households and married taxpayers with two or more exemptions.

Tax Table D Selection

The section of Tax Table D to be used is based on Marital Status.

Step 11. Type In and Press Enter:

```
4450 ON M GOTO 4460,4480,4500
4460 REM  Single Person Tax Table D - Biweekly
4480 REM  Married Person Tax Table D - Biweekly
4500 REM  Head of House Tax Table D - Biweekly
```

M   Marital Status

Line 4450 selects the appropriate section of Tax Table D based on the value recorded in the Variable M.

The structure of these tables is the same as the federal Tax Tables explained on pages 98 to 100.

```
                      BI-WEEKLY PAYROLL PERIOD
============================================================

                        SINGLE TAXPAYERS

  If The Taxable
     Income Is...      The Computed Tax Is..          Or
                      --------------------        --------------
   Over   But Not     Of Amount       Plus        Amount  Minus
           Over        Over...                     Times

      0    119...   1 %       0 +     0.00       1 %  -     0.00
    119    207...   2 %     119 +     1.19       2 %  -     1.19
    207    296...   3 %     207 +     2.96       3 %  -     3.25
    296    386...   4 %     296 +     5.62       4 %  -     6.22
    386    475...   5 %     386 +     9.22       5 %  -    10.08
    475    565...   6 %     475 +    13.68       6 %  -    14.82
    565    653...   7 %     565 +    19.04       7 %  -    20.51
    653    742...   8 %     653 +    25.20       8 %  -    27.04
    742    831...   9 %     742 +    32.34       9 %  -    34.44
    831    920...  10 %     831 +    40.37      10 %  -    42.73
    920 And Over. 11 %     920 +    49.26      11 %  -    51.94
------------------------------------------------------------
```

Step 12. Type In and Press Enter:

```
4461 IF S = <119 THEN ST(E) = 1/100 * S:GOTO 4520
4462 IF S = <207 THEN ST(E) = 2/100 * S - 1.19:GOTO 4520
4463 IF S = <296 THEN ST(E) = 3/100 * S - 3.25:GOTO 4520
4464 IF S = <386 THEN ST(E) = 4/100 * S - 6.22:GOTO 4520
4465 IF S = <475 THEN ST(E) = 5/100 * S - 10.08:GOTO 4520
4466 IF S = <565 THEN ST(E) = 6/100 * S - 14.82:GOTO 4520
4467 IF S = <653 THEN ST(E) = 7/100 * S - 20.51:GOTO 4520
4468 IF S = <742 THEN ST(E) = 8/100 * S - 27.04:GOTO 4520
4469 IF S = <831 THEN ST(E) = 9/100 * S - 34.44:GOTO 4520
4470 IF S = <920 THEN ST(E) = 10/100 * S - 42.73:GOTO 4520
4471 ST(E) = 11/100 * S - 51.94:GOTO 4250
```

```
                    MARRIED TAXPAYERS                                    UNMARRIED HEADS OF HOUSEHOLDS

 If The Taxable                                         If The Taxable
   Income Is...    The Computed Tax Is..       Or         Income Is...    The Computed Tax Is..       Or
                  -----------------------  ------------                 -----------------------  ------------
 Over  But Not    Of Amount       Plus     Amount  Minus   Over  But Not    Of Amount       Plus     Amount  Minus
        Over      Over...                  Times                  Over      Over...                  Times

    0    238...   1 %       0 +    0.00    1 %  -    0.00     0    238...   1 %       0 +    0.00    1 %  -    0.00
  238    415...   2 %     238 +    2.38    2 %  -    2.38   238    356...   2 %     238 +    2.38    2 %  -    2.38
  415    592...   3 %     415 +    5.92    3 %  -    6.53   356    445...   3 %     356 +    4.74    3 %  -    5.94
  592    772...   4 %     592 +   11.25    4 %  -   12.43   445    534...   4 %     445 +    7.43    4 %  -   10.37
  772    951...   5 %     772 +   18.45    5 %  -   20.15   534    623...   5 %     534 +   10.98    5 %  -   15.72
  951  1,129...   6 %     951 +   27.37    6 %  -   29.69   623    713...   6 %     623 +   15.44    6 %  -   21.94
1,129  1,305...   7 %   1,129 +   38.08    7 %  -   40.95   713    802...   7 %     713 +   20.80    7 %  -   29.11
1,305  1,484...   8 %   1,305 +   50.41    8 %  -   53.99   802    890...   8 %     802 +   27.02    8 %  -   37.14
1,484  1,662...   9 %   1,484 +   64.68    9 %  -   68.88   890    980...   9 %     890 +   34.12    9 %  -   45.98
1,662  1,840...  10 %   1,662 +   80.75   10 %  -   85.45   980  1,068...  10 %     980 +   42.15   10 %  -   55.85
1,840 And Over.  11 %   1,840 +   98.52   11 %  -  103.88 1,068 And Over.  11 %   1,068 +   51.04   11 %  -   66.44
```

Step 13. Type In and Press Enter:

```
4481 IF S = <238 THEN ST(E) = 1/100 * S:GOTO 4520
4482 IF S = <415 THEN ST(E) = 2/100 * S - 2.38:GOTO 4520
4483 IF S = <592 THEN ST(E) = 3/100 * S - 6.53:GOTO 4520
4484 IF S = <772 THEN ST(E) = 4/100 * S - 12.43:GOTO 4520
4485 IF S = <951 THEN ST(E) = 5/100 * S - 20.15:GOTO 4520
4486 IF S = <1129 THEN ST(E) = 6/100 * S - 29.69:GOTO 4520
4487 IF S = <1305 THEN ST(E) = 7/100 * S - 40.95:GOTO 4520
4488 IF S = <1484 THEN ST(E) = 8/100 * S - 53.99:GOTO 4520
4489 IF S = <1662 THEN ST(E) = 9/100 * S - 68.88:GOTO 4520
4490 IF S = <1840 THEN ST(E) = 10/100 * S - 85.45:GOTO 4520
4491 ST(E) = 11/100 * S - 103.88:GOTO 4250
```

Step 14. Type In and Press Enter:

```
4501 IF S = <238 THEN ST(E) = 1/100 * S:GOTO 4520
4502 IF S = <356 THEN ST(E) = 2/100 * S - 2.38:GOTO 4520
4503 IF S = <445 THEN ST(E) = 3/100 * S - 5.94:GOTO 4520
4504 IF S = <534 THEN ST(E) = 4/100 * S - 10.37:GOTO 4520
4505 IF S = <623 THEN ST(E) = 5/100 * S - 15.72:GOTO 4520
4506 IF S = <713 THEN ST(E) = 6/100 * S - 21.94:GOTO 4520
4507 IF S = <802 THEN ST(E) = 7/100 * S - 29.11:GOTO 4520
4508 IF S = <890 THEN ST(E) = 8/100 * S - 37.14:GOTO 4520
4509 IF S = <980 THEN ST(E) = 9/100 * S - 45.98:GOTO 4520
4510 IF S = <1068 THEN ST(E) = 10/100 * S - 55.85:GOTO 4520
4511 ST(E) = 11/100 * S - 66.44:GOTO 4250
```

California Tax Credit Table

Tax Table C uses the number of Tax Exemptions to determine a credit that can be subtracted from the tax due. One set of tables is for single taxpayers and the other Tax Table is for married taxpayers and heads of households.

```
                        TABLE C - TAX CREDIT TABLE

PAYROLL PERIOD
-----------------------------------------------------------------------------------
  MARITAL    /                    ALLOWANCES ON DE-4 OR W-4                    10 OR
  STATUS     /  0      1      2      3      4      5      6      7      8      9 MORE+
-----------------------------------------------------------------------------------
  BIWEEKLY
    SINGLE     0.00   1.50   1.90   2.40   2.80   3.30   3.80   4.20   4.70   5.20   5.60
    OTHER*     0.00   1.50   2.90   3.40   3.80   4.30   4.80   5.20   5.70   6.20   6.60
-----------------------------------------------------------------------------------
*   MARRIED OR UNMARRIED HEADS OF HOUSEHOLDS.

+   IF THE NUMBER OF ALLOWANCES CLAIMED EXCEEDS 10, YOU MAY DETERMINE THE AMOUNT OF TAX
    CREDIT TO BE ALLOWED BY MULTIPLYING THE DIFFERENCE BETWEEN THE AMOUNTS SHOWN FOR 9 AND
    "10 OR MORE" ALLOWANCES BY THE NUMBER OF ALLOWANCES CLAIMED IN EXCESS OF 10 AND THEN
    ADDING TO THIS PRODUCT THE AMOUNT SHOWN FOR "10 OR MORE" ALLOWANCES.
```

Step 15. Type In and Press Enter:

```
4520 ON M GOTO 4530,4550,4550
4530 REM  Single Tax Credit Table C – Biweekly
4550 REM  Other Tax Credit Table C – Biweekly
```

Line 4520 selects the appropriate table based on the Marital Status recorded in the Variable M.

Step 16. Type In and Press Enter:

```
4531 IF X = 0 THEN GOTO 4590
4532 ON X GOTO 4535,4536,4537,4538,4539,4540,4541,4542,4543
4533 GOTO 4544
4535 ST(E) = ST(E) – 1.5 : GOTO 4590
4536 ST(E) = ST(E) – 1.9 : GOTO 4590
4537 ST(E) = ST(E) – 2.4 : GOTO 4590
4538 ST(E) = ST(E) – 2.8 : GOTO 4590
4539 ST(E) = ST(E) – 3.3 : GOTO 4590
4540 ST(E) = ST(E) – 3.8 : GOTO 4590
4541 ST(E) = ST(E) – 4.2 : GOTO 4590
4542 ST(E) = ST(E) – 4.7 : GOTO 4590
4543 ST(E) = ST(E) – 5.2 : GOTO 4590
4544 ST(E) = ST(E) – (5.6 + (X – 10) * .4) : GOTO 4590
```

Lines 4531 to 4533 use the number of Tax Exemptions to direct the program to the line containing the appropriate tax credit. For example, if one tax exemption is claimed, X=1, the program proceeds to Line 4535.

Lines 4535 to 4544 deduct the tax credit, with Line 4544 deducting the credit for ten or more exemptions.

```
                    TABLE C - TAX CREDIT TABLE
PAYROLL PERIOD
-------------------------------------------------------------------
  MARITAL    /              ALLOWANCES ON DE-4 OR W-4
  STATUS     /  0     1     2     3     4     5     6     7     8     9   10 OR
-------------------------------------------------------------------------MORE+
  BIWEEKLY
    SINGLE      0.00  1.50  1.90  2.40  2.80  3.30  3.80  4.20  4.70  5.20  5.60
    OTHER*      0.00  1.50  2.90  3.40  3.80  4.30  4.80  5.20  5.70  6.20  6.60
-------------------------------------------------------------------------
*  MARRIED OR UNMARRIED HEADS OF HOUSEHOLDS.

+  IF THE NUMBER OF ALLOWANCES CLAIMED EXCEEDS 10, YOU MAY DETERMINE THE AMOUNT OF TAX
   CREDIT TO BE ALLOWED BY MULTIPLYING THE DIFFERENCE BETWEEN THE AMOUNTS SHOWN FOR 9 AND
   "10 OR MORE" ALLOWANCES BY THE NUMBER OF ALLOWANCES CLAIMED IN EXCESS OF 10 AND THEN
   ADDING TO THIS PRODUCT THE AMOUNT SHOWN FOR "10 OR MORE" ALLOWANCES.
```

Step 17. Type In and Press Enter:

```
4551 IF X = 0 THEN GOTO 4590
4552 ON X GOTO 4555,4556,4557,4558,4559,4560,4561,4562,4563
4553 GOTO 4564
4555 ST(E) = ST(E) - 1.5 : GOTO 4590
4556 ST(E) = ST(E) - 2.9 : GOTO 4590
4557 ST(E) = ST(E) - 3.4 : GOTO 4590
4558 ST(E) = ST(E) - 3.8 : GOTO 4590
4559 ST(E) = ST(E) - 4.3 : GOTO 4590
4560 ST(E) = ST(E) - 4.8 : GOTO 4590
4561 ST(E) = ST(E) - 5.2 : GOTO 4590
4562 ST(E) = ST(E) - 5.7 : GOTO 4590
4563 ST(E) = ST(E) - 6.2 : GOTO 4590
4564 ST(E) = ST(E) - (6.6 + (X - 10) * .4) : GOTO 4590
```

Lines 4551 to 4564 determine the tax credit for married taxpayers and heads of households the same way Lines 4531 to 4544 determine the credit for single taxpayers.

Completing the State Tax Calculation

The State Income Tax deduction must be rounded off to the nearest cent. If a negative deduction has been created, it must be set to zero.

Step 18. Type In and Press Enter:

```
4590 ST(E) = INT(100 * ST(E) + .5)/100
4595 IF ST(E) < 0 THEN ST(E) = 0
```

Line 4590 rounds off the tax withholding to the nearest cent.
Line 4595 sets the value of negative deductions to zero.

NET PAY

The Net Pay is determined by subtracting the deductions from the Gross
Pay. The result is recorded in the Array NP( ).

Step 19. Type In and Press Enter:

```
4600 REM  Calculate Net Pay
4610 NP(E) = GP(E) – FT(E) – SS(E) – ST(E) – SD(E)
RUN
```

FT( )	Federal Tax
GP( )	Gross Pay
NP( )	Net Pay
SD( )	State Disability Insurance
SS( )	Social Security Withholding
ST( )	State Tax

Expanding Information Storage

The values generated by the calculations can now be recorded on Disk or
Cassette Tape for later use by the totaling program.

Step 20. Type In and Press Enter:

```
8100 PRINT#1,RE(N),OE(N),FT(N),SS(N)
8110 PRINT#1,ST(N),SD(N),NP(N)
9100 INPUT#1,RE(N),OE(N),FT(N),SS(N)
9110 INPUT#1,ST(N),SD(N),NP(N)
```

Extending the Employee List

The current Payroll Program is limited to processing ten employees. This
number can be increased by using a DIM Instruction to specify a larger size for the
Arrays used to record the information about each employee.

Step 21. Type In and Press Enter:

```
600 W = 3:REM  Total Number of Employees for This Year
610 DIM GP(W),W1(W),W2(W)
620 DIM RT(W),OT(W),RE(W),OE(W)
630 DIM FT(W),SS(W),ST(W),SD(W),NP(W)
```

Line 600 is already a part of the program. It specifies the number of employees in the
current list.

Lines 610 to 630 place each of the Arrays used in the program in a DIM Instruction.
The DIM Instruction establishes the maximum number of Variables within an Array.
When the value of the Variable W is used, the Arrays are set to the number of
employees being processed.

Basic Printing Functions

There are two basic types of printed forms: records of individual transactions and summaries of multiple transactions. In business, individual transactions are recorded on receipts, invoices, and checks, while a summary form is represented by a profit and loss statement. In education, report cards reflect transactions while grade sheets summarize the information. In the home, a name and address can be the basis for a transaction with an address list being the summary. The two forms described for the Payroll Program are the Paycheck and the Payroll Summary.

The structure of the record of an individual transaction is different from the structure of a summary report. The records of individual transactions are designed to be passed from one party to another. For example, the employer passes paychecks to the employees. Both parties of the transaction need to be clearly indicated on the form. That is why a paycheck includes the employee number, name, and Social Security number. The employer is identified as well by name, address, and authorized signature. In addition, the terms of the transaction need to be clearly defined. For example, a paycheck stub will include a list of every item used to calculate the Gross Pay as well as every deduction that determines the Net Pay.

Summary reports record a series of transactions. These summaries are usually retained only by the party initiating the transaction. Therefore, it is not necessary to delineate each party in the transaction as explicitly as it is for records of individual transactions. For example, a payroll summary may contain just the employee number and name. Similarly, if the summaries are used strictly for in-house accounting, there is no need to put the company name or address on the form. The primary function of the summary is to give an overall view of transactions that have occurred. More than one report might be used to clarify the elements of the transactions. For example, the payroll summary may include columns of information for Gross Pay, FIT, FICA, SIT, SDI, and Net Pay. If additional deductions or sources of income are included, there may be too much information to put on one page. One form could record a summary of the combined information necessary to create the Gross Pay, such as hours worked, rate of pay, regular hours, overtime hours, bonuses. A second form could summarize all the information about deductions. A third form could indicate the Gross Pay totaled from summary one, the deductions totaled from summary two, and the resulting Net Pay. The exact structure of these forms must be adjusted to suit the requirements of the parties using the forms. However, the information should always be printed in a format that makes it useful.

While the structure of the record for a single transaction is different from the summary report, certain print routines perform basic functions that are essential to both types of forms. Other print routines also use a similar structure to print information in a variety of different formats.

To simplify the process of creating print routines for virtually any type of form, this section separates each identifiable function into a separate subroutine. The routines for any given form can then be created by mixing and matching the subroutines described below.

BASIC SUBROUTINES

Open a Communication Channel – The program must open a channel of communication to the printer, since the output from a program is normally directed to the display unless otherwise specified.

Output a Line to the Printer – The PRINT Instruction displays information on the screen. A variation of this instruction is used to direct a line of copy to the printer.

Close the Communication Channel – After the information has been printed, the program must close the communication channel to the printer.

Interrupt Control – A printer may run out of paper or ribbon or the paper may jam. When this happens, the Operator must be able to stop the output to the printer.

FORMAT SUBROUTINES

Vertical Tab – A line must sometimes be printed at a certain vertical position on the form. The vertical tab subroutine directs the printer to this location. This is particularly important when preprinted forms such as paychecks are being completed.

Horizontal Tabs – The horizontal position for printing each piece of data must be established. This position may be in relation to the left, center, or right side of the information to be printed.

Dollar Format – The computer does not store monetary information in the usual written format. For example, zeros following the last significant digit on the right side of the decimal are dropped. Dollar signs are also not stored with monetary data. A subroutine therefore needs to be used to create the correct format for monetary values.

SIMILAR SUBROUTINES

Sequence of Items in a Line – Each form requires a different sequence of information to be printed in any given line. While each line may be different, the basic concept of tabbing to individual items in a line allows a similar structure to be used regardless of the specific content.

Sequence of Lines on a Page – The patterns of lines on a page can vary. For records of individual transactions, it is possible that no two lines will have the same information. In this case, the placement and content of each line must be specified. On the other hand, summaries of transactions usually contain information printed in columns. The individual lines follow the same format but print different data.

This chapter describes the subroutines used with all print routines. The chapter starting on page 117 describes how these routines can be used to print records of individual transactions. The chapter starting on page 126 describes how they can be used to print summaries of transactions.

To test the subroutines in this chapter, temporary program lines are included. These program lines will be deleted after the routines have been tested.

Output to the Printer

A communication channel must be opened to the printer. Individual lines of copy can then be directed to the printer. After all the copy has been printed, the communication channel must be closed. Three separate subroutines perform these functions.

Step 1.   Type In and Press Enter:

```
5 GOTO 280
130 OPEN "LPT1:" AS #2:WIDTH#2,255
135 RETURN
140 PRINT#2,P$:REM   Alternate: 140 PRINT#2,P$;CHR$(10)
145 PL = PL + 1:RETURN
150 CLOSE#2
155 RETURN
```

PL   Number of Lines Printed

Line 5, which begins the program, directs it to the first line that is not a subroutine.

Line 130 opens the communication channel to the first parallel printer port, "LPT1:". This can be changed to the second parallel printer port or a serial port depending on the printer being used. Communication channel #2 is used for output to the printer. The WIDTH Instruction in this line suppresses the Line Feed that is normally added when the copy is printed.This subroutine is used before a form or series of forms is to be printed.

Lines 140 and 145 direct the printer to print an individual line of copy. The information to be printed is recorded in the Variable P$. An alternate version of Line 140 is given which issues a Line Feed, CHR$(10), after each line is printed. If the printer does not advance the paper up out of the printer after printing it, this variation of Line 140 should be used.

Line 145 adds a value of one to the Variable PL for every line that is printed. This allows the program to keep track of the number of lines printed on the current page.

Line 150 closes communication channel #2.

Interrupt Control

The interrupt control can be used by the Operator to stop output from going to the printer. This action is required when the paper is in crooked or in the wrong location, when the printer runs out of paper or ribbon, or when the paper jams.

The interrupt control monitors input from the Keyboard. If the Space Bar is pressed, the value in an Interrupt Variable is changed. This changed value is used by other routines in the program to change the direction the program follows. If the Space Bar is not pressed, the program follows the normal sequence for printing a form.

Step 2. Type In and Press Enter:

```
120 IN = 0:A$ = INKEY$:IF A$ = " " THEN IN = 1
125 RETURN
```

In Line 120, the Variable IN is the interrupt control. The value of this Variable is set to zero. The INKEY$ Instruction scans the Keyboard and returns the character of any key depressed to the Variable A$. The IF THEN Instruction then determines if the Space Bar, A$=" ", has been pressed. If it has, the value of the Variable IN is changed to one.

Vertical Tab Control

The vertical tab control advances the paper up out of the printer. This control is required when information must be printed at a certain distance from the top of the page. Frequent use of this control is required for preprinted forms such as paychecks.

Step 3. Type In and Press Enter:

```
160 D = VT - PL:IF D <1 THEN RETURN
170 P$ = " ":FOR A =1 TO D:GOSUB 140:NEXT A:RETURN
```

D	Distance for Paper to Advance
PL	Number of Lines Printed
VT	Vertical Tab Position

Line 160 determines the distance the printer is to advance the paper. The position the printer must advance to is recorded in the Variable VT. The current position of the printer is recorded in the Variable PL. The difference between these two positions is recorded in the Variable D. If this is not a value of at least one, the subroutine is terminated with the RETURN Instruction.

Line 170 advances the paper out of the printer by setting the line to be printed as a space, P$=" ". The FOR NEXT Loop is then used to send the correct number of blank lines to the printer, GOSUB 140.

The following temporary lines will test this routine.

> **Step 4.   Temporary Lines.   Type In and Press Enter:**
>
> ```
> 400 GOSUB 130
> 410 P$ = "Begin Test":GOSUB 140
> 420 VT = 6:GOSUB 160
> 430 P$ = "End Test":GOSUB 140
> 440 GOSUB 150
> 450 END
> RUN
> ```

Line 410 prints a line of copy to begin the test.

Line 420 specifies a Vertical Tab six lines down from the top of the page.

Line 430 prints a line of copy to end the test so that the actual distance the printer travels can be seen.

Formatting Dollars

The computer does not store numeric values in a dollar format. For example, if a value of one dollar is recorded by a program, the computer remembers this as 1, not 1.00. Similarly, a dollar and ten cents is recorded as 1.1, not 1.10.

In order to express monetary values in a dollar format, the numeric monetary values must be converted to a String expression of the number. This String expression can then be adjusted to include the appropriate dollar format.

> **Step 5.   Type In and Press Enter:**
>
> ```
> 5920 A = INT(100 * V + .5)/100:VA$ = STR$(A):VI$ = STR$(INT(A))
> 5930 IF LEN(VA$) = LEN(VI$) THEN VA$ = VA$ + "."
> 5940 L = LEN(VI$) + 3:IF A > 0 AND A < 1 THEN L = L − 1
> 5950 VA$ = VA$ + "00":A$ = A$ + MID$(VA$,2,L − 1)
>
> V = 1.1:A$ = "":GOSUB 5920:PRINT A$
> ```

In Line 5920, the Variable V introduces the value that must be converted to the dollar format. The first instruction in this line rounds off the value of the Variable V to the nearest cent. (This formula is described in detail on page 95.) The next instruction converts the value in the Variable A to a String representation of the rounded-off value using the STR$ Instruction. This String representation is retained in the Variable VA$. The final instruction in this line records a String representation of the integer of the number in the Variable VI$. Thus, if the value of the Variable V is 1.1, the contents of the Variable VA$ will be "1.1" and the contents of the Variable VI$ will be "1".

Line 5930 determines if the length of the value is the same length as the integer of the value. This is accomplished by the LEN Instruction which counts the number of characters in a String Variable. The two Variables will be the same length when an even dollar amount has been recorded. If this is the case, there will be no decimal point in the Variable VA$ so a decimal point is added.

Line 5940 establishes the number of characters that must be present to represent the dollar format. This is calculated by taking the length of the integer String (the whole dollar amount) and adding a value of three (one decimal point and two digits for cents). The last instruction in Line 5940 determines if the value being processed is less than a dollar. When this is the case, the Variable VA$ might have a value of ".5" and the Variable VI$ would have a value of "0". If three digits are added to the length of the Variable VI$, the resulting String would be four characters long creating ".500" instead of ".50". To correct this, the length of the format recorded in the Variable L is reduced by one, L=L–1.

Line 5950 adds two zeros to the end of the Variable VA$. This means that a value of 1.1 would now be recorded in the Variable VA$ as "1.100". To adjust the contents of the Variable VA$ to the correct dollar format, the MID$ Instruction is used. This instruction starts from the second character of the Variable VA$ and counts over one less than the number of characters recorded in the Variable L. Anything that exceeds this length is eliminated. The program starts counting from the second character because of the space added to the beginning of positive numbers by the computer. The value in the Variable L is also reduced by one to adjust for this length.

The following steps indicate what happens when a value of 1.1 is recorded in the Variable V. For clarity, String values are indicated between quotation marks, numeric values are not.

1. Initial Value: V= 1.1
2. 5920 A=INT(100*V+.5)/100: A= 1.1
3.   VA$=STR$(A): VA$=" 1.1"
4.   VI$=STR$(INT(A)): VI$=" 1"
5. 5930 IF LEN(VA$)=LEN(VI$) THEN: No action taken
6. 5940 L=LEN(VI$)+3: L=5
7.   IF A>0 AND A<1 THEN: No action taken
8. 5950 VA$=VA$+"00": VA$=" 1.100"
9.   A$=A$+MID$(VA$,2,L–1): A$="1.10" (4 characters)

The results of this routine can be tested by typing in sample values as indicated in the last line of Step 5. These values can be tested without running the program.

Horizontal Tabs

Horizontal tabs place the items of data to be printed in their correct location within the line of copy. These tabs add spaces to the line between the items to be printed, building each line from left to right. As each new item is added to a line, a calculation is made to determine how many spaces must be added to the current line to achieve the tab position for the new item.

The Payroll Program uses two types of tabs. One tab specifies the distance from the left margin to the left side of the item to be added. The other tab specifies the distance from the left margin to the right side of the item to be added. This second tab is required so that columns of monetary values can be printed with the decimal points aligned. Because the dollar format always has two digits to the right of the decimal point but any number of digits to the left, a tab to the right must be specified to maintain the correct alignment.

Within the tab to the right there are three variations. One prints the dollar format without a dollar sign. The second prints the dollar format with a dollar sign. And the third variation tabs to the right side of the item without creating the dollar format at all. This tab can be used to add headings above columns of numbers.

The following lines create these different formats.

Step 6. Type In and Press Enter:

```
300  FOR A = 1 to 120 : SP$ = SP$ + " " : LN$ = LN$ + " – " : NEXT A
5900 A$ = SP$ : GOTO 5920 : REM  Tab Right with Dollar Format
5910 A$ = SP$ + "$" : REM  Tab Right with "$"
5950 VA$ = VA$ + "00" : A$ = A$ + MID$(VA$,2,L – 1)
5960 P$ = LEFT$(P$,TB) : TB = TB – LEN(P$)
5970 P$ = P$ + RIGHT$(A$,TB) : RETURN
5980 A$ = SP$ + A$ : GOTO 5960 : REM  Tab Right.  No Dollar Format
5990 P$ = P$ + SP$ : P$ = LEFT$(P$,TB) + A$ : RETURN : REM  Tab Left
```

SP$	Line of Spaces
LN$	Line of Hyphens
TB	Horizontal Tab

In Line 300, a FOR NEXT Loop creates a line of spaces in the Variable SP$ and a line of hyphens in the Variable LN$.

Line 5900 begins the subroutine for the dollar format. It prepares the Variable A$ with a line of spaces. The program is then directed to Line 5920, which begins the dollar format routine.

Line 5910 begins the subroutine for the dollar format. It adds a line of spaces with a dollar sign to the Variable A$. The program drops from this line to the beginning of the dollar format.

Line 5950 from Step 5 is repeated here. It ends the dollar format routine by adding the String of the dollar value, VA$, to the current contents of the Variable A$. When the program proceeds from Line 5900, the Variable A$ contains a line of spaces. When the program proceeds from Line 5910, the Variable A$ contains a line of spaces followed by a dollar sign. The monetary value of the Variable VA$ is added immediately after the dollar sign.

Lines 5960 and 5970 add the new value to be tabbed to the current line.

Line 5960 first uses the LEFT$ Instruction to shorten the current line in the Variable P$ to the new tab position. This step is a safety check that should not affect the line if the tabs have been correctly determined. The length of the information to be tabbed is then determined by subtracting the length of the current line from the specified tab position, TB=TB − LEN(P$).

Line 5970 uses the RIGHT$ Instruction to shorten the contents of the Variable A$ to the correct length.

As an example of how these two lines work, assume the current line recorded in the Variable P$ is 30 characters long and the new value, recorded in the Variable A$, is to be tabbed to 50. The LEFT$ Instruction in Line 5960 does not change the contents of the Variable P$ because the value of TB is greater than the length of the current line. The value of the Variable TB is then reduced by the length of the Variable P$ to 20, 50-30=20. Line 5970 shortens the contents of the Variable A$ to 20 characters and adds this to the current contents of the Variable P$. The contents of the Variable P$ is now 50 characters, which is the tab length initially specified.

Line 5980 begins the subroutine that sets an item with a right tab without going through the dollar format routine.

Line 5990 is the tab subroutine for tabs to the left side of an item. This line first adds the line of spaces to the existing line of copy in the Variable P$. The length of the Variable P$ is then shortened to the specified tab position using the LEFT$ Instruction. To this is added the current item stored in the Variable A$.

Testing the Horizontal Tab

The horizontal tab routines can be tested by adding the following temporary lines to the program.

Step 7. Type In and Press Enter:

```
400 P$="":V=12.34:TB=15:GOSUB 5900:PRINT P$
410 V=56.78:TB=25:GOSUB 5910:PRINT P$
420 P$="":A$="Test Left":TB=5:GOSUB 5990
430 A$="Test Right":TB=35:GOSUB 5980:PRINT P$
440 END
RUN
```

TB	Horizontal Tab
V	Value to be Formatted

Step 8. The Computer Displays:

```
          12.34
          12.34    $56.78
Test Left          Test Right
```

Line 400 clears the Variable P$ to start a new line of copy. A value of 12.34 is assigned to the Variable V and a horizontal tab of 15 is assigned to the Variable TB. The subroutine starting at Line 5900 is used to create the dollar format. The results of the line appear as the first line in Step 8.

Line 410 changes the value in the Variable V to 56.78 and the tab to 25. The program is then directed to the subroutine starting at Line 5910, which adds the dollar sign to the dollar format. The results are seen in the second line of step 8. The value from Line 400 is still a part of the line because the Variable P$ was not cleared at the beginning of Line 410. This illustrates how lines of copy can be built using different values and different tab stops until the desired format is achieved.

Line 420 clears the Variable P$ and sets the phrase "Test Left" at a tab of five. The subroutine starting at Line 5990 uses the left side of the item as the reference for the tab location.

Line 430 tests the subroutine that uses the right tab without the dollar format.

The four formats illustrated in these lines can now be used to create any layout desired.

Printing Records of Transactions

The Paycheck is a good example of a record of an individual transaction. No two lines on the check contain the same information. In addition, this type of check can be purchased on continuous form paper so that all the checks can be printed without Operator intervention.

To prepare a printing routine for this type of form, follow the steps described below.

1. Write in the information to be printed on a copy of the form.

2. Determine the horizontal and vertical position of each item of information.

3. Develop the routines for printing each individual line of copy and test for accuracy.

4. After the routine to complete the form is developed, create a FOR NEXT Loop to process all of the transactions.

The following description applies this procedure to the creation of the print routine for Paychecks.

Evaluating the Form

The first step in developing the print routine is to evaluate the form to be printed. The information to be printed on the form should be written in by hand. Then the vertical and horizontal position of each piece of data can be determined.

Vertical and Horizontal Starting Point – A vertical and horizontal starting point must be established first. All other tab measurements are taken from these reference points.

The Programmer's Reference Guide shown on page 118 indicates how these points can be established. The top perforation of the form is used as the vertical reference point. The left edge of the paper is used as the horizontal reference line. This may need to be adjusted for the printer being used. For example, when the printer is initially turned on, the print head may settle at the perforations on the form instead of at the left edge of the paper. When this is the case, the horizontal reference numbers should be cut from the form and moved to the location best suited to the printer. In this example, the horizontal reference line is changed to start from the perforations on the form instead of the left edge of the paper.

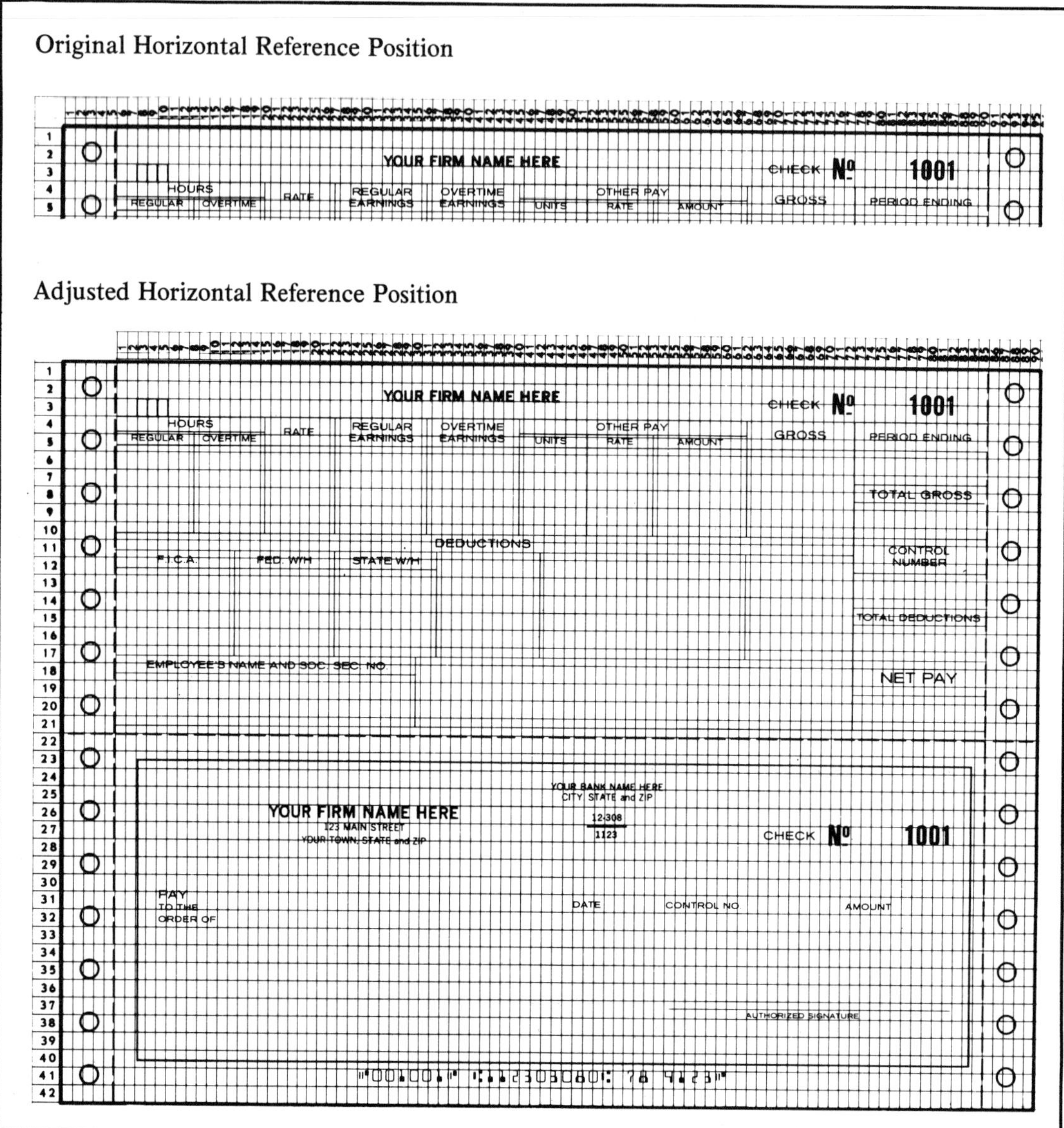

Programmer's Reference Guide

Programer's Reference Guide courtesy of NEBS Computer Forms

Establishing a logical vertical and horizontal starting point is important because these will be the marks the Operator will use to adjust the forms in the printer. If the marks are arbitrary, there is a good chance that the Operator will misalign the forms. However, if placement of the forms is established logically, the chances are better that the paper will always be correctly positioned in the printer.

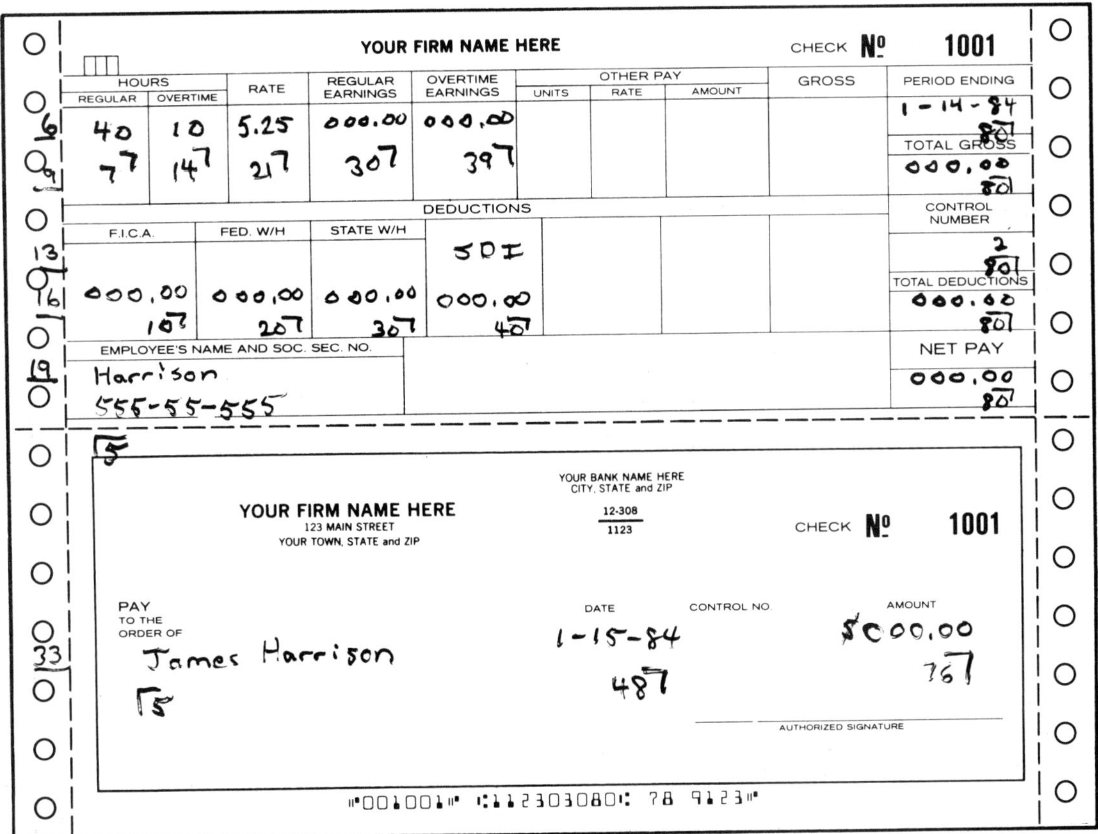

Marked Paycheck

Paycheck courtesy of NEBS Computer Forms

Vertical and Horizontal Tabs – The tab position for each item of data can now be given a vertical and horizontal reference measurement.

If a Programmer's Reference Guide is being used, the values for these measurements can be read directly from this form. If a reference guide is not available, the measurements can be determined using a forms ruler which is available from most stationery stores. These rulers divide horizontal lines into 10 spaces per inch and vertical lines into 6 lines per inch. This spacing increment is commonly used by printers. The forms ruler numbers the spaces sequentially across the full length of the ruler, which is usually as long as the widest paper used in a printer.

The vertical and horizontal measurements can be marked directly on the copy of the form that has been completed by hand. These marks should clearly indicate whether a left or right tab is to be used. An example of a marked form is indicated above.

With the form prepared in this manner, the print routine can easily be developed by indicating the data, tab measurements, and tab subroutines for each item.

The Initial Position

The initial control indicates how much the printer must advance the paper to reach the first line to be printed. It is possible that the form cannot be easily positioned in the printer so that the vertical reference line of the form is directly under the print head. If this is the case, an alignment point must be established using some mark on the print-head carriage mechanism or the top of the print wheel guard. The position of the paper in relation to the vertical reference line must then be indicated.

Step 1. Type In and Press Enter:

```
5500 VS = 2 : PL = VS : REM  Starting Line
5510 VT = 6 : GOSUB 160 : REM  First Vertical Line
5515 GOSUB 120 : IF IN = 1 THEN RETURN
```

IN	Interrupt Control
PL	Number of Lines Printed
TB	Horizontal Tab
VS	Vertical Starting Position
VT	Vertical Tab

Line 5500 establishes the vertical starting position in the Variable VS. This value is then transferred to the Variable PL. For this example, the form is placed so that the second line of the form is positioned level with the print wheel. This value may need to be adjusted for the specific printer being used.

Line 5510 directs the program to the vertical tab routine, GOSUB 160, to advance the paper to the sixth line on the form, VT=6.

Line 5515 directs the program to the interrupt control. If the Operator presses the Space Bar immediately after the print routine starts, the value in the Variable IN will be set to one and the printing will be discontinued.

Printing Information about Earnings

The first line of copy on the Paycheck is the description of the employee's earnings. This includes the hours, rate of pay, earnings, and ending date of the Pay Period.

Step 2. Type In and Press Enter:

```
5520 P$ = "" : A$ = STR$(RT(E)) : TB = 7 : GOSUB 5980 : REM  Reg. Time
5530 A$ = STR$(OT(E)) : TB = 14 : GOSUB 5980 : REM  Overtime
5540 V = P : TB = 21 : GOSUB 5900 : REM  Rate of Pay
5550 V = RE(E) : TB = 30 : GOSUB 5900 : REM  Regular Earnings
5560 V = OE(E) : TB = 39 : GOSUB 5900 : REM  Overtime Earnings
5570 A$ = ED$ : TB = 83 : GOSUB 5980 : REM  Period Ending
5580 GOSUB 140 : VT = 9 : GOSUB 160
5585 GOSUB 120 : IF IN = 1 THEN RETURN
5795 RETURN
```

TB	Horizontal Tab
V	Value to be Formatted

Lines 5520 to 5570 establish the information to be printed on the first line of the form. The REM Instructions indicate exactly which item is being added to the line.

Line 5520 clears the print Variable P$ to begin a new line. The STR$ Instruction then converts the numeric value of the Regular Hours Worked, RT(E), to a String expression. The tab is set to seven, TB=7, and the program is directed to the subroutine which sets non-dollar information with a right tab, GOSUB 5980.

Line 5530 performs the same function as Line 5520, but the Overtime Hours, OT(E), are used and the tab is advanced to 14.

Line 5540 retrieves the rate of pay from the Variable P, then sets the tab to 21 and directs the program to the subroutine that creates the dollar format.

Lines 5550 and 5560 add the regular and overtime earnings to the line using the dollar format.

Line 5570 adds the ending date of the Pay Period to the line.

Line 5580 directs the program to the subroutine that prints the current line of copy, GOSUB 140. A vertical tab then advances the form to the ninth line, VT=9:GOSUB 160.

Line 5795 terminates the printing of an individual Paycheck.

Testing the Print Routine

The following temporary lines can be added to the program to test the printing of the Paycheck as this routine is developed.

```
Step 3.  Temporary Lines.  Type In and Press Enter:

400 W1(1) = 35:W2(1) = 45:ED$ = "4 - 1 - 84"
410 GOSUB 9500:GOSUB 4000
420 GOSUB 130:GOSUB 5500:GOSUB 150
430 END
RUN
```

Line 400 enters temporary data into the program so the print routine will print actual values.

Line 410 directs the program to the subroutine that retrieves the employee information, GOSUB 9500. The program is then directed to the subroutine that calculates the payroll information, GOSUB 4000.

Line 420 directs the program to the subroutine that opens the communication channel to the printer, GOSUB 130. The current Paycheck information is then printed, GOSUB 5500. Finally, the communication channel to the printer is closed, GOSUB 150.

During the testing stage, blank paper can be used in the printer. This paper can then be held up in front of the Paycheck form to determine if the information has been printed in the correct location. A full-sized copy of the Paycheck described here is included in Appendix B.

Gross Pay & Employee Number

The next two lines to be printed only contain a few items. The positions of these lines are primarily determined by the boxes on the right hand side of the form.

```
Step 4.   Type In and Press Enter:

5600 P$ = "":V = GP(E):TB = 83:GOSUB 5900:REM  Gross Pay
5610 GOSUB 140:VT = 13:GOSUB 160
5615 GOSUB 120:IF IN = 1 THEN RETURN
5620 P$ = "":A$ = "SDI":TB = 40:GOSUB 5980:REM  SDI Label
5630 A$ = STR$(E):TB = 80:GOSUB 5980:REM  Employee Number
5640 GOSUB 140:VT = 16:GOSUB 160
5645 GOSUB 120:IF IN = 1 THEN RETURN
```

Lines 5600 to 5615 are used to print the Gross Pay in the box marked Total Gross. Line 5610 then advances the printer to line 13 on the form.

Lines 5620 to 5645 print the SDI deduction label in the fourth column of the form and indicate the Employee Number in the left box titled "Control Number." Line 5640 advances the printer to line 16 on the form.

The Deduction Line

The deduction line is similar in format to the earnings line.

```
Step 5.   Type In and Press Enter:

5650 P$ = "":V = SS(E):TB = 10:GOSUB 5900:REM  FICA
5660 V = FT(E):TB = 20:GOSUB 5900:REM  FIT
5670 V = ST(E):TB = 30:GOSUB 5900:REM  SIT
5680 V = SD(E):TB = 40:GOSUB 5900:REM  SDI
5690 V = SS(E) + FT(E) + ST(E) + SD(E):TB = 80:GOSUB 5900
5700 GOSUB 140:VT = 19:GOSUB 160
5705 GOSUB 120:IF IN = 1 THEN RETURN
RUN
```

Lines 5650 to 5680 prepare the line of copy for the four basic deductions after Line 5650 first clears the print Variable P$.

Line 5690 is slightly different in that it totals the deductions in the Variable V before adding this information to the line of copy.

Line 5700 is used to print the copy and advance the printer to line 19 of the form.
Line 5705 is the interrupt control.

This much of the program should be run to test this portion of the print routine.

Completing the Paycheck Stub

The Paycheck stub is completed by printing the employee's name and Social Security number and the Net Pay.

```
Step 6.  Type In and Press Enter:

       5710 P$ = "":A$ = F$ + " " + N$:TB = 5:GOSUB 5990:REM Name
       5720 GOSUB 140
       5725 GOSUB 120:IF IN = 1 THEN RETURN
       5730 P$ = "":A$ = S$:TB = 5:GOSUB 5990:REM  Soc. Sec. #
       5740 V = NP(E):TB = 80:GOSUB 5900:REM  Net Pay
       5750 GOSUB 140:VT = 33:GOSUB 160
       5755 GOSUB 120:IF IN = 1 THEN RETURN
```

Line 5710 prepares the employee's name by adding the first name, F$, to the last name, N$. The tab is set to five and the left tab subroutine is used, GOSUB 5990.

Line 5720 prints the current line but does not use a vertical tab because the next line of copy is to appear on the next line of the form.

Line 5730 prepares the next line of copy by adding the Social Security number of the employee.

Line 5740 adds the Net Pay to the line.

Line 5750 is used to print the line and advance the printer to the thirty-third line of the form.

Body of the Check

The main body of the Paycheck has only three items of data: the employee's name, the current date, and the Net Pay.

```
Step 7.  Type In and Press Enter:

       5760 P$ = "":A$ = F$ + " " + N$:TB = 5:GOSUB 5990:REM Name
       5770 A$ = TD$:TB = 48:GOSUB 5980:REM  Today's Date Number
       5780 V = NP(E):TB = 76:GOSUB 5910:REM  Net Pay
       5790 GOSUB 140:VT = 42 + VS:GOSUB 160
       5795 RETURN
       RUN
```

Lines 5760 to 5780 prepare the copy for the body of the check.

Line 5790 is used to print this line of copy and then advance the check out of the printer so the next check can be printed. The vertical tab control is a combination of the length of the check form, 42, plus the vertical starting position established in Line 5500, +VS.

When this much of the program is run, the complete check will be printed.

Processing the Employees

A FOR NEXT Loop can now be used so that Paychecks for each of the employees can be printed.

```
Step 8.   Type In and Press Enter:

5050 GOSUB 130:RESTORE:REM  Initialize Printer
5060 FOR N = 1 TO W
5070 GOSUB 9500:REM  Retrieve Employee Information
5080 IF C < 1 OR NP(E) = 0 THEN GOTO 5100
5090 GOSUB 5500:IF IN = 1 THEN GOTO 5110
5100 NEXT N
5110 GOSUB 150:RETURN
```

    C   Employee Code
NP( ) Net Pay

Line 5050 opens the communication channel to the printer before any check is processed.

Lines 5060 to 5100 form the FOR NEXT Loop that processes each employee. These lines are similar to the FOR NEXT Loops that have been used to display information.

Line 5080 bypasses the printing of a Paycheck when the Net Pay, NP(E), is zero.

Line 5090 directs the program to print a Paycheck, GOSUB 5500, then determines if the interrupt control has been activated, IN=1.

Line 5110 closes the communication channel to the printer and returns the program to the menu.

Prompting the Operator

The last function to be added to this routine is a prompt that alerts the Operator to check the condition of the printer and make sure the correct forms are in place.

```
Step 9.   Type In and Press Enter:

5000 CLS: REM  Alternate:  5000 PRINT CHR$(12);
5010 PRINT TAB(D1 + 6);"PREPARE TO PRINT PAY CHECKS":PRINT
5020 PRINT TAB(D1 + 3);"IS THE PRINTER READY ( <Y> OR N)";
5030 A$ = "":INPUT A$:IF A$ = "N" OR A$ = "n" THEN RETURN
5040 PRINT TAB(D1 + 5);"TO STOP PRINTER PRESS (SPACE)"
```

Lines 5000 and 5010 clear the screen and inform the Operator that this routine is used to print Paychecks.

Lines 5020 and 5030 are the pause control that allows the Operator the option to abort this routine.

Line 5040 is the prompt that reminds the Operator how to stop the printer by using the interrupt control if necessary.

Running the Program

The program can now be run to test the full check-printing routine. But the temporary Lines 400 to 450 must first be deleted from the program so the routines can be processed in the correct sequence.

Step 10. Type In and Press Enter:
400
410
420
430
440
450
RUN

Printing a Transaction Summary

The Payroll Summary form is a good example of a summary of a series of transactions. The routine for this type of form is similar in structure to the display routines described earlier. The form begins with a heading that indicates the information being summarized. This is followed by a series of columns that lists the information from each transaction. The bottom of the form can be completed with a total of the information in each column. Ideally, summaries should be self-contained on a single sheet of paper for easy correlation and review.

To prepare a routine for this type of form, the steps described below should be followed.

1. Prepare a copy of the form by hand to determine what information needs to be printed and where it is to be placed on the page.

2. Determine the horizontal position where the data is to be printed. After an initial vertical tab down from the top of the paper, the lines of information will occur sequentially, so no additional vertical tabs should be required.

3. Develop the routine for printing the heading for the form.

4. Develop the routine to print the columns of information.

5. Add a FOR NEXT Loop to process all of the transactions.

6. Add the routines which will total the information and print it at the bottom of the columns.

The following discussion applies this procedure to a routine to print the Payroll Summary.

Creating the Form

Summaries should print information in a form that is meaningful to the people who need to evaluate the data. Good guidelines for creating the layout for these forms can be determined by evaluating the forms used for manual tabulations.

The first factor to consider is what size paper the form is to be printed on. The following details affect this decision.

1. What is the maximum size of the paper the printer can handle? Some printers will take paper up to 14-inches wide while other printers are limited to 8-1/2 inches.

2. How many characters can the printer produce in a single line of copy? Normal pica type prints 10 characters per inch. Most printers also handle elite type at 12 characters per inch or condensed print at 15 or 17 characters per inch.

If a different horizontal pitch, such as elite, is to be used, how difficult is it to change the character font? If a daisywheel printer is being used, it can be inconvenient to change from a pica printwheel to an elite printwheel for just one form.

3. What size paper will all the other forms be printed on? If multiple summaries are going to be retained, standardizing the paper size is a good idea. It is a nuisance to have most information on 8-1/2-inch paper and one form on 14-inch paper as the two different sizes do not fit conveniently in a single size binder.

4. What direction is the type to run on the paper? Usually it is easier to use 8-1/2-by-11-inch paper vertically. Sometimes, however, the information is easier to follow if the paper is used horizontally. In this case, it is necessary to determine how convenient it will be to place the information in the printer. For example, if a tractor feed is set up to handle 8-1/2-inch-wide continuous forms, it may be difficult to insert a single 11-inch form in the printer.

After the paper size has been determined, a sample form should be prepared by hand. This form should include all of the different items of information to be printed and the tabs for each item should be established. Indicated below is the Payroll Summary form described in this section. This form is designed to use 8-1/2-by-11-inch paper in the horizontal direction. It requires a printer which can handle at least 105 characters per line. If this width cannot be handled, the deductions can be summarized on a separate form and entered here as a total.

The routines for printing this form can now be developed.

Initial Layout

Printed Version

```
                                PAYROLL SUMMARY
                     For Pay Period # 1   Ending 1-14-84

    #    Name           Reg Earn   OT Earn     Gross        FIT       FICA        SIT       SDI     Net Pay

    1    Harrison, J.     393.75     23.63     417.38      46.17      27.96       6.66      3.76      332.83
    2    Samuels, B.      440.00     41.25     481.25      37.89      32.24       1.22      4.33      405.57
    3    Johnson, L.      362.25      0.00     362.25      23.20      24.27       0.00      3.26      311.52
                     ------------------------------------------------------------------------------------
                     $ 1196.00  $ 64.88 $ 1260.88  $ 107.26   $ 84.47    $ 7.88   $ 11.35 $ 1049.92
```

Payroll Summary

Summary Heading

The summary heading describes the overall contents of the form with a subheading that specifies the date of the current summary. For this summary, the headings are centered.

```
              Step 1.   Type In and Press Enter:

            6500 VS = 2 : PL = VS : REM  Starting Line
            6510 VT = 6 : GOSUB 160 : REM  First Vertical Line
            6515 GOSUB 120 : IF IN = 1 THEN RETURN
            6520 P$ = "" : A$ = "PAYROLL SUMMARY"
            6530 TB = INT((110 - LEN(A$)) / 2) : GOSUB 5990
            6540 GOSUB 140 : GOSUB 120 : IF IN = 1 THEN RETURN
            6550 P$ = "" : A$ = "For Pay Period # " + PP$ + "  Ending " + ED$
            6560 TB = INT((110 - LEN(A$)) / 2) : GOSUB 5990
            6570 GOSUB 140 : GOSUB 120 : IF IN = 1 THEN RETURN
            6580 P$ = " " : GOSUB 140
```

IN	Interrupt Control
PL	Number of Lines Printed
TB	Horizontal Tab
VS	Vertical Starting Position
VT	Vertical Tab

Line 6500 indicates the starting location of the paper. For this example, the paper is positioned so that the print head is level with the second line of the paper.

Line 6510 uses a vertical tab of six lines or one inch to create a top margin for the form.

Line 6520 creates the main heading for the form.

Line 6530 calculates a tab that will center the heading on the paper. The calculation subtracts the length of the heading, LEN(A$), from the total width of the paper in characters, 110. The result of this subtraction is then divided by two to determine how many spaces must be added to the beginning of the line. This value is used with the tab left subroutine, GOSUB 5990.

Line 6540 prints the heading.

Lines 6550 to 6570 center the subheading that identifies the number of the Pay Period, PP$, and the ending date of the Pay Period, ED$. Without this identifying subhead, it would not be possible to distinguish one Pay Period summary from another.

Line 6580 adds a blank line between the main headings and the column headings.

Column Headings

The column headings indicate the specific content within each column. The tabs used for this heading are identical to the tabs for the information in the columns.

```
Step 2.  Type In and Press Enter:

6600 P$ = "" : A$ = " #" : TB = 5 : GOSUB 5990
6610 A$ = "Name" : TB = 10 : GOSUB 5990
6620 A$ = "Reg Earn" : TB = 35 : GOSUB 5980
6630 A$ = "OT Earn" : TB = 45 : GOSUB 5980
6640 A$ = "Gross" : TB = 55 : GOSUB 5980
6650 A$ = "FIT" : TB = 65 : GOSUB 5980
6660 A$ = "FICA" : TB = 75 : GOSUB 5980
6670 A$ = "SIT" : TB = 85 : GOSUB 5980
6680 A$ = "SDI" : TB = 95 : GOSUB 5980
6690 A$ = "Net Pay" : TB = 105 : GOSUB 5980
6695 GOSUB 140 : P$ = " " : GOSUB 140 : GOSUB 120 : RETURN
```

Lines 6600 to 6690 build the line of column headings.

Line 6695 is used to print the line and adds a blank line between the column heading and the first line of data.

Prompting the Operator

The basic sequence of lines that alert the Operator to prepare the printer can now be added.

Step 3.   Type In and Press Enter:

```
6000 CLS: REM  Alternate:  6000 PRINT CHR$(12);
6010 PRINT TAB(D1 + 4);"PREPARE TO PRINT PAYROLL SUMMARY"
6020 PRINT TAB(D1 + 3);"IS THE PRINTER READY ( <Y> OR N)";
6030 A$ = "":INPUT A$:IF A$ = "N" OR A$ = "n" THEN RETURN
6040 PRINT TAB(D1 + 5);"TO STOP PRINTER PRESS (SPACE)"
6050 GOSUB 130:RESTORE:PL = 0:REM  Initialize Printing
6270 IF PL>0 THEN GOTO 6290
6280 GOSUB 6500:IF IN = 1 THEN GOTO 6370:REM  Print Heading
6370 GOSUB 150:RETURN
```

Lines 6000 and 6010 clear the screen and alert the Operator that the Payroll Summary is to be printed.

Lines 6020 and 6030 are the pause control that also allows the Operator to abort the printing.

Line 6050 initializes the communication with the printer.

Lines 6270 and 6280 are used to print the heading, GOSUB 6500. The control of Variable PL bypasses the heading after it is printed once, PL>0. This is similar to the way the display routines skip the heading after it is initially displayed.

Line 6370 terminates the print routine.

Condensed Printing

Some Dot Matrix printers, such as the Epson RX-10, will only print an 80-column line unless they are sent a special software control. This software control allows the selection of either elite or condensed type. When this type of printer is used, the software control should be sent immediately after the communication channel to the printer is opened for the summary form. For this example, the type is changed to the condensed face so the full 105 characters of the summary can be printed.

Step 4.   Epson Printer.   Type In and Press Enter:

```
5051 P$ = CHR$(18):GOSUB 140:PL = 0
6051 P$ = CHR$(15):GOSUB 140:PL = 0
```

Line 5051 is added to the check-printing routine to ensure that the printer is in the pica width for this form.

Line 6051 uses the command to set condensed type, CHR$(15), in the Variable P$ which is then printed. The number of lines printed must be adjusted to zero as this is a control line rather than an actual line of print.

When this control is added to the form, the vertical starting position recorded in Lines 5500 and 6500 may have to be adjusted because it advances the paper by one line. For example, if the initial starting position recorded in the Variable VS is two, it must be increased to three.

Test Printing the Heading

The following temporary lines can be added to the program to test the printing of the headings. After the test is run, these lines should be deleted.

```
Step 5.   Temporary Lines.   Type In and Press Enter:

          400 PP$ = "8":ED$ = "4 – 1 – 84"
          420 GOSUB 6000
          430 END
          RUN
          400
          420
          430
```

Printing the Data

Now that the headings have been printed, the data for each employee can be processed.

```
Step 6.   Type In and Press Enter:

          6700 P$ = "":A$ = STR$(E):TB = 5:GOSUB 5990:REM  Employee #
          6710 A$ = N$ + ", " + LEFT$(F$,1) + ".":REM  Employee Name
          6715 TB = 10:GOSUB 5990
          6720 V = RE(E):TB = 35:GOSUB 5900:REM  Regular Earnings
          6730 V = OE(E):TB = 45:GOSUB 5900:REM  Overtime Earnings
          6740 V = GP(E):TB = 55:GOSUB 5900:REM  Gross Pay
          6750 V = FT(E):TB = 65:GOSUB 5900:REM  FIT
          6760 V = SS(E):TB = 75:GOSUB 5900:REM  FICA
          6770 V = ST(E):TB = 85:GOSUB 5900:REM  SIT
          6780 V = SD(E):TB = 95:GOSUB 5900:REM  SDI
          6790 V = NP(E):TB = 105:GOSUB 5900:REM  Net Pay
          6795 GOSUB 140:GOSUB 120:RETURN
```

Lines 6700 to 6795 follow the same format for printing the data as Lines 6600 to 6695 used to print the column headings. The only difference is that monetary values are used and printed using the dollar format, GOSUB 5900.

Processing the Employees

A FOR NEXT Loop can now be established to process the information for each employee.

```
Step 7.   Type In and Press Enter:

      6260 FOR N = 1 TO W
      6290 GOSUB 9500 : REM   Retrieve Employee Information
      6300 IF C < 1 OR GP(E) = 0 THEN GOTO 6360
      6310 GOSUB 6700 : IF IN = 1 THEN GOTO 6370 : REM   Print Wages
      6360 NEXT N
      RUN
```

C   Employee Code

Lines 6260 to 6360 use the same format as the display routine to process the information for each employee. Line 6310 directs the program to the subroutine that prints the data for an individual employee.

Totaling the Information

The information for the employees can be added together to provide an overall total.

```
Step 8.   Type In and Press Enter:

      6255 RE = 0 : OE = 0 : GP = 0 : FT = 0 : SS = 0 : ST = 0 : SD = 0 : NP = 0
      6304 RE = RE + RE(E) : OE = OE + OE(E) : GP = GP + GP(E)
      6306 FT = FT + FT(E) : SS = SS + SS(E) : ST = ST + ST(E)
      6308 SD = SD + SD(E) : NP = NP + NP(E)
      6365 GOSUB 6800 : REM   Print Totals
```

Line 6255 clears the Variables that record the totals before the **FOR NEXT** Loop starts processing the individual employees.

Lines 6304 to 6308 total the information for each column of data.

Line 6365 directs the program to the routine that prints the total.

Printing the Total

The total is printed following the same sequence of lines used to print the rest of the information in the columns.

Step 9. Type In and Press Enter:

```
6800 P$ = "":A$ = LEFT$(LN$,80):TB = 105:GOSUB 5980:REM  Line
6810 GOSUB 140:GOSUB 120:IF IN = 1 THEN RETURN
6820 P$ = "":V = RE:TB = 35:GOSUB 5910:REM  Regular Earnings
6830 V = OE:TB = 45:GOSUB 5910:REM  Overtime Earnings
6840 V = GP:TB = 55:GOSUB 5910:REM  Gross Pay
6850 V = FT:TB = 65:GOSUB 5910:REM  FIT
6860 V = SS:TB = 75:GOSUB 5910:REM  FICA
6870 V = ST:TB = 85:GOSUB 5910:REM  SIT
6880 V = SD:TB = 95:GOSUB 5910:REM  SDI
6890 V = NP:TB = 105:GOSUB 5910:REM  Net Pay
6895 GOSUB 140:RETURN
RUN
```

Lines 6800 and 6810 print a line of hyphens at the bottom of the columns.

Lines 6820 to 6895 follow the same sequence of lines found in Steps 3 and 6 for printing the column headings and the data within the columns.

Changing the Paper

If many transactions are being recorded, the information may not fit on a single sheet of paper. A pause control must therefore be added to warn the Operator to put in a new sheet.

Step 10. Type In and Press Enter:

```
6320 IF PL <51 − 6 THEN GOTO 6360
6330 PRINT:PRINT TAB(D1 + 6);"PUT IN A NEW SHEET OF PAPER"
6340 PRINT TAB(D1 + 6);"TO CONTINUE PRESS (ENTER)";
6350 INPUT A$:PL = 0
```

PL   Number of Lines Printed

Line 6320 records the length of the paper being used. In this case, 8-1/2-by-11-inch paper is being used, so the length of the paper is 8.5 times 6 lines per inch, or 51 lines of printing. A value of 6 is subtracted from this amount to leave a 1-inch margin at the bottom of the paper.

Lines 6330 to 6350 are the pause control that warns the Operator to change the paper. When the Operator signals that a new sheet of paper has been inserted by pressing the Enter Key, the value in the Variable PL is set to zero. This causes the heading to be printed on the new sheet of paper, see Step 3 on page 130.

When continuous-form paper is used, the following line can be substituted so that no action on the part of the Operator is required.

> **Step 11. Continuous Forms. Type In and Press Enter:**
>
> 6325 VT = 51 + VS : GOSUB 160 : PL = 0 : GOTO 6360

    PL   Number of Lines Printed
    VS   Vertical Starting Position
    VT   Vertical Tab

Line 6325 uses a vertical tab that is the depth of the paper plus the value of the Variable VS which indicates the vertical starting position.

Program Documentation

After a program has been developed, it is helpful to describe its design. Such notes simplify the process of adding new features and modifying existing routines at a later time. The notes need not be lengthy descriptions on a line-by-line basis. However, they should include an outline of the program lines, a listing of each routine in the program, a table of the Variables, and instructions for the Operator.

An Outline of Program Lines

The functions of the program and their respective Line Numbers should be listed. This outline serves as a Table of Contents for the program. An example of this type of outline is shown for the Payroll Program on page 136.

In this outline, every major block of program lines is indicated. In addition, each subroutine that is referred to from some other part of the program is identified. For example, all of the subroutines that control the operation of the printer are listed.

The outline should also contain a detailed breakdown of the program lines that may need to be altered, such as the Tax Tables and employee records.

```
                    PROGRAM LINE DESCRIPTION
                      the Payroll Program

  Initial Subroutines                          120-170
     Printer Interrupt                         120-125
     Open for Printer Output                   130-135
     Output a Line to the Printer              140-145
     Close Output to Printer                   150-155
     Vertical Tab for Printer                  160-170
  Initial Program Lines                        280-700
     Initial Prompts                           500-560
     DIM Instructions                          600-630
  Main Menu                                    800-990
  Entry Routine                               1000-1410
  Display Routines                            2000-2650
     Display Hours & Gross Pay                 2000-2150
     Display Earnings & Deductions             2200-2370
     Display Employee Records                  2500-2650
  Correct Hours                               3000-3590
     Correct Hours of Individual               3500-3590
  Calculations  (Update Annually)             4000-4690
     Calculate Overtime                        4030-4090
     FICA Withholding                          4100-4140
     California SDI                            4150-4190
     FIT Withholding                           4200-4255
        Withholding Allowance                     4220
        Tax Table 2a - Single                  4230-4238
        Tax Table 2b - Married                 4240-4248
     California SIT                            4400-4595
        Withholding Allowance                  4410-4450
        Tax Table D - Single                   4460-4471
        Tax Table D - Married                  4480-4491
        Tax Table D - Head of Household          4500-4511
        Tax Credit - Single                    4530-4544
        Tax Credit - Other                     4550-4564
     Net Pay                                   4600-4690
  Print Paychecks                             5000-5795
     Body of Check                             5500-5795
  Horizontal Tabs                             5900-5990
     Tab Right - Dollar Format                    5900
     Tab Right - Dollar Format + $                5910
     Tab Right - No Dollar Format                 5980
     Tab Left  - No Dollar Format                 5990
  Print Payroll Summary                       6000-6895
     Headings                                  6500-6695
     Data in Columns                           6700-6795
     Totals                                    6800-6895
  Store Payroll                               8000-8280
     Store Earnings & Deductions               8000-8140
     Store Pay Period Number                   8250-8280
  Retrieval Routines                          9000-9630
     Retrieve Payroll Data                     9000-9150
     Retrieve Pay Period                       9200-9280
     Retrieve Employee Data                    9500-9510
     Employee Records                          9600-9630
        (Adjust to Change Employee Status)
```

Program Listings

All of the program lines should be printed. The program should be broken down so individual functions are printed on separate pages.

The following lines show how the entry routine, Lines 1000-1410, can be printed.

Type In and Press Enter:
LLIST 1000 – 1999

Notes about the program's operation can be added to these listings. For example, the horizontal tabs for the print routines can be used in a wide variety of programs. The description of these routines should include the Variables that need to be given values before the subroutine is used, the format of the line that directs the program to the subroutine, and the Variable that returns the results of the routine.

Table of Variables

A careful record should be maintained for the names of all of the Variables and Arrays. This allows new Variables to be added without interfering with the function of existing Variables.

If a program line is used to assign an important value to a Variable, the Line Number should be included in the table.

A sample Table of Variables for the Payroll Program is shown below.

```
                        TABLE OF VARIABLES

     A   -  Operator Response          PL   -  Number of Lines Printed
     A$  -  Operator Response, String          (Adjusted in Line 145)
     C   -  Employee Code              PP$  -  Number of Pay Period
     D   -  Number of Lines Displayed          (Set in Line 560)
     D1  -  Display Tab for Centering   RE   -  Regular Earnings, Total
            (Set in Line 280)         RE( ) -  Regular Earnings
     D3  -  Depth of Video Screen      RT( ) -  Regular Hours
            (Set in Line 290)          S    -  Taxable Income, State
     E   -  Employee Number             S$   -  Social Security Number
     ED$ -  Ending Date of Pay Period   SD   -  State Disability, Total
            (Set in Line 550)         SD( ) -  State Disability Insurance
     F   -  Taxable Income, Federal     SP$  -  Line of Spaces
     F$  -  First Name                  SS   -  Social Security, Total
     FT  -  Federal Tax, Total         SS( ) -  Social Security Withholding
   FT( ) -  Federal Tax                 ST   -  State Tax, Total
     GP  -  Gross Pay, Total           SS( ) -  State Tax
   GP( ) -  Gross Pay                   T    -  Total Gross Pay
     IN  -  Interrupt Control           TB   -  Horizontal Tab
            (GOSUB 120)                 TD$  -  Current Date
     L   -  Length of String                  (Set in Line 540)
     LN$ -  Line of Hyphens             V    -  Value of Dollar Format
     M   -  Marital Status              VA$  -  String of Dollar Value
     N   -  Counter for FOR NEXT Loops  VI$  -  String of Integer of Dollar
     N$  -  Name                        VS   -  Vertical Starting Location
     NP  -  Net Pay, Total              VT   -  Vertical Tab
   NP( ) -  Net Pay                     W    -  Number of Workers
     OE  -  Overtime Earnings, Total           (Set in Line 600)
   OE( ) -  Overtime Earnings          W1( ) -  Hours for Week One
   OT( ) -  Overtime Hours             W2( ) -  Hours for Week Two
     P   -  Rate of Pay                 WK   -  Week to be Changed
     P$  -  Line to be Printed          X    -  Number of Tax Exemptions
```

Operator's Instructions

Operator's instructions should be created to describe the operation of the program. This information should be compiled as the program is run.

The description of the program's operation should include every step that must be performed, including putting in the Disk and turning on the computer. Steps for the operation of the print routines should indicate how the paper is to be aligned in the printer. A simple illustration or copy of the form should be used.

When a prompt changes the direction of the program, each option should be described. An example for the Payroll Program is indicated below.

```
    6.  The next prompt that appears is "Correct These Hours (Y
or <N>)?"
    A "Yes" response to this prompt directs the program to a
routine that allows the hours to be changed.  Select this option
by pressing the "Y" Key followed by the Return/Enter Key.
    A "No" response allows the next employee to be entered.
Select this option by pressing the "N" Key followed by the
Return/Enter Key.  This response may also be selected by
pressing the Return/Enter Key.
```

Creating the Operator's Instructions serves two purposes. First, it informs someone who has never used the program how to operate it. It also determines whether the operation of the program follows a logical sequence. If the instructions take the Operator through a convoluted sequence of steps to accomplish a simple task or asks an unnecessary question, the program may need to be redesigned.

To evaluate the design, the purpose of each prompt should be questioned as it may be possible to establish the information automatically without having to bother the Operator. For example, in the current Payroll Program, an initial question requests "Today's Date." The IBM PC has a built-in calendar function. The program can be converted to establish the date automatically. Indicated below is an example of this modification. for the IBM

Step 1. Type In and Press Enter:

```
540 TD$ = DATE$
```

Optimum efficiency of the program's design can only be attained by critically evaluating every step the Operator must perform.

The Summary Program

Summary Programs total the information produced from multiple runs of programs that process individual transactions.

For a Summary Program, the Operator usually only has to enter the date the program is being run. The remainder of the input comes from the output of the transaction programs that have been recorded on a magnetic storage device. The primary manipulation of the input data is to total the information.

The output for a Summary Program can either be a display on the Video Screen or a printout. The Summary Program can also be used to convert the information into data that another program can use for input. This allows information from various tasks to be correlated into significant reports. For example, the Payroll Program generates data biweekly. The Payroll Summary Program can total this information for a given month, quarter, or year. The totals can then be entered as an expense item in a general ledger program for the development of profit and loss statements and financial position reports. To develop routines for this type of output, it is necessary to understand the input requirements of the general ledger program. For this reason, the discussion in this book will concentrate on printed output reports.

The two output reports developed in this chapter total the information for each employee, then total the information for all employees. Both reports allow options for summarizing the data monthly, quarterly, and/or yearly. The reports for individual employees show the employee's name in the heading and list all wages by Pay Period. The Summary Report for all employees follows the same format as the one used in the Payroll Program.

Data for Summary Programs

The main consideration for a Summary Program is the vast amount of information that must be processed. For example, in the Payroll Program eight different Arrays were used to record the information about earnings, deductions, and Net Pay. The Payroll Summary Program must retain the eight different pieces of data for as many as 26 different biweekly Pay Periods. This is a total of 208 different items of data for each employee.

To store this information in a fashion that is easy to understand, a two-dimensional Array is used, such as GP(E,PP) for Gross Pay. This type of Array uses two Variables between the parentheses to record different locations in the computer's memory. When either of the values in these Variables is changed, a different location in the computer's memory is referenced. In this way, the Variable E can be used to record the current employee and the Variable PP can be used to record the current Pay Period. The chart below illustrates the different memory locations in the computer's memory for a two-dimensional Array.

GP(E,PP)	GP(E,1)	GP(E,2)	GP(E,3)
GP(1,PP) GP(2,PP) GP(3,PP)	GP(1,1) GP(2,1) GP(3,1)	GP(1,2) GP(2,2) GP(3,2)	GP(1,3) GP(2,3) GP(3,3)

Two Dimensional Array

Adapting the Payroll Program

Other than this one change in the way information is stored in the Arrays, the remainder of the Payroll Summary Program uses the retrieval and printing routines already described. Thus, the easiest way to develop the Payroll Summary Program is to save the current copy of the Payroll Program; modify it by deleting routines not required for the Summary Program; then add the new routines; and save the resulting program with a different file name.

The program lines indicated in Step 1 will not be used for the Payroll Summary Program. These lines should be deleted after the Payroll Program has been saved using the DELETE Instruction.

Step 1. Type In and Press Enter:

```
DELETE 810-890
DELETE 1000-5795
DELETE 8000-8140
```

Retrieving Data

The retrieval routine must follow exactly the same sequence of instructions as the storage function in the Payroll Program. The only change is using the new Arrays to recover the information.

```
Step 2.   Type In and Press Enter:

      9060 INPUT#1,ED$(PP)
      9090 INPUT#1,A,A,GP(N,PP)
      9100 INPUT#1,RE(N,PP),OE(N,PP),FT(N,PP),SS(N,PP)
      9110 INPUT#1,ST(N,PP),SD(N,PP),NP(N,PP)
```

Line 9060 retrieves the ending date of the Pay Period in an Array so that each Pay Period is retrieved with an identifying date.

Line 9090 retrieves three data items. The first two items record the hours worked. This particular information will not be used in the current program so a dummy Variable A is used. The Gross Pay is then retrieved in the Array GP(N,PP).

Lines 9100 and 9110 retrieve the information for earnings and deductions in Arrays that can keep track of the information for each employee by Pay Period.

Preparing the Arrays

The Arrays must be prepared with a DIM Instruction to specify the number of items to be used.

```
Step 3.   Type In and Press Enter:

      600 W = 3: REM   Total Number of Employees for This Year
      610 DIM GP(W,26),ED$(26)
      620 DIM RE(W,26),OE(W,26),FT(W,26)
      630 DIM SS(W,26),ST(W,26),SD(W,26),NP(W,26)
      640 DIM TR(W),TE(W),TG(W),TF(W),TS(W)
      650 DIM TX(W),TD(W),TN(W)
```

In Lines 610 to 650, the DIM Instruction specifies that 26 Pay Periods need to be processed. When a weekly Pay Period is used, this value is increased to 52. When a monthly pay period is used, the quantity is reduced to twelve. The Variable W records the number of employees to be processed.

Retrieving All the Data

A FOR NEXT Loop retrieves the information for each Pay Period, from the beginning of the year through the last payroll processed.

```
Step 4.  Type In and Press Enter:

      560 GOSUB 9200:PE=VAL(PP$)
      700 CLS: REM  Alternate:  700 PRINT CHR$(12);
      710 PRINT TAB(D1+6);"DO NOT DISTURB, I'M WORKING"
      720 FOR PP=1 TO PE
      730 PP$=MID$(STR$(PP),2)
      740 GOSUB 9040:REM  Retrieve Payroll
      750 NEXT PP
```

Line 560 directs the program to the subroutine that retrieves the number for the last Pay Period processed, GOSUB 9200. This value is recorded in the Variable PP$. This String value is converted to a numeric value which is then recorded in the Variable PE.

Lines 700 and 710 clear the screen and alert the Operator that the computer will be accessing the storage device and should not be disturbed.

Lines 720 to 750 form a FOR NEXT Loop that retrieves all of the payroll data from the first of the year to the last Pay Period entered, PE.

Line 730 converts the numeric value of the current Pay Period, PP, to the String representation of the number. This string is part of the file name used to retrieve the date. If the computer being used does not add a space to the beginning of positive numbers, the program should be changed as indicated for the Apple II.

Line 740 directs the program to the subroutine that retrieves the payroll data. The program is directed to Line 9040 rather than Line 9000 because Line 9000 starts the retrieval with a pause control. Line 9040 begins the actual retrieval.

Cassette Tape Conversion

Cassette Tape systems require a slight change to this routine. The subroutine starting at Line 9200 automatically retrieves the file that records the last Pay Period entered. However, this file is not available in a Cassette Tape system, so the information must be entered manually.

```
Step 4.  Cassette Conversion.  Type In and Press Enter:

      560 PRINT "ENTER # OF LAST PAY PERIOD";:INPUT PE
      725 IF PP=1 THEN GOSUB 9000:GOTO 750
```

Line 560 adds an INPUT Instruction to determine the number of the last Pay Period entered.

Line 725 is added to the FOR NEXT Loop so the program will proceed to the prompt that warns the Operator to make sure the equipment is ready. This step is only performed for the first Pay Period, PP=1. This line is not required for Disk systems which have an equivalent prompt starting at Line 9200.

SUMMARY BY EMPLOYEE

To prepare a summary which indicates the wages of an employee by Pay Period, some additional routines must be added to the existing program. The program must also be extended so that the summary can be made on a monthly, quarterly, or yearly basis.

Adjusting the Headings

The same structure for the routine that prints the headings for the original summary is used, but the subheading is changed to the employee's name. Also, the first column heading is changed from Employee Number to Pay Period number. The second column heading is changed from Employee Name to the ending date of the Pay Period.

Step 5. Type In and Press Enter:

```
7500 VS = 2:PL = VS:REM  Starting Line
7510 VT = 6:GOSUB 160:REM  First Vertical Line
7515 GOSUB 120:IF IN = 1 THEN RETURN
7520 P$ = "":A$ = "PAYROLL SUMMARY FOR: " + F$ + " " + N$
7530 TB = INT((110 – LEN(A$))/2):GOSUB 5990
7540 GOSUB 140:GOSUB 120:IF IN = 1 THEN RETURN
7580 P$ = " ":GOSUB 140
7600 P$ = "":A$ = " #":TB = 5:GOSUB 5990
7610 A$ = "Ending Date":TB = 10:GOSUB 5990
7620 GOSUB 6620:RETURN
```

Lines 7500 to 7515 and Lines 7530 to 7600 are identical to Lines 6500 to 6600 of the Payroll Program, see page 128.

Line 7520 changes the main heading by adding the first and last names of the employee, F$+" "+N$.

Lines 7600 and 7610 change the first two column headings from the Employee Number and name to the Pay Period and ending date.

Line 7620 directs the program to Line 6620, which adds the rest of the column headings from the existing routines and prints this line of copy.

Changing Data Arrays

The data to be printed in the summary must be taken from the new Arrays used by the retrieval routine.

```
Step 6.   Type In and Press Enter:

7700 P$ = "" : A$ = STR$(PP) : TB = 5 : GOSUB 5990 : REM  Pay Period
7710 A$ = ED$(PP) : TB = 10 : GOSUB 5990 : REM  Ending Date
7720 V = RE(E,PP) : TB = 35 : GOSUB 5900 : REM  Regular Earnings
7730 V = OE(E,PP) : TB = 45 : GOSUB 5900 : REM  Overtime Earnings
7740 V = GP(E,PP) : TB = 55 : GOSUB 5900 : REM  Gross Pay
7750 V = FT(E,PP) : TB = 65 : GOSUB 5900 : REM  FIT
7760 V = SS(E,PP) : TB = 75 : GOSUB 5900 : REM  FICA
7770 V = ST(E,PP) : TB = 85 : GOSUB 5900 : REM  SIT
7780 V = SD(E,PP) : TB = 95 : GOSUB 5900 : REM  SDI
7790 V = NP(E,PP) : TB = 105 : GOSUB 5900 : REM  Net Pay
7795 GOSUB 140 : GOSUB 120 : RETURN
```

Line 7700 is changed to use the Pay Period number, PP, as the first item to be printed in the line.

Line 7710 uses the ending date to identify the payroll data in the remainder of the line.

Lines 7720 to 7795 are identical to Lines 6720 to 6795 for the original Payroll Program, except the data is extracted from the new Arrays.

Processing the Data

The lines that direct the program to the headings and data follow the same structure as Lines 6260 to 6360 in the Payroll Program, see pages 130 to 133.

```
Step 7.   Type In and Press Enter:

6060 FOR N = 1 TO W
6070 GOSUB 9500 : REM  Retrieve Employee Information
6080 IF PL > 0 THEN GOTO 6100
6090 GOSUB 7500 : IF IN = 1 THEN GOTO 6370 : REM  Print Heading
6100 FOR PP = 1 TO PE
6110 GOSUB 7700 : IF IN = 1 THEN GOTO 6370 : REM  Print Wages
6120 NEXT PP
6160 NEXT N
```

Lines 6060 to 6160 form the FOR NEXT Loop that processes each of the employees.

Line 6070 retrieves the record for the employee being processed.

Lines 6080 and 6090 are used to print the heading at the top of the paper.

Lines 6100 to 6120 form a FOR NEXT Loop that prints all of the data for each Pay Period for the employee being processed.

Selecting Summary Period

The initial program menu is adjusted to allow the Operator to select the type of summary to be printed: monthly, quarterly, or yearly.

```
Step 8.    Type In and Press Enter:

810 PRINT TAB(D1 + 7); "PAYROLL SUMMARY FUNCTIONS"
820 PRINT TAB(D1 + 7); "-------------------------"
830 PRINT TAB(D1 + 6); "1) PRINT MONTH'S SUMMARY"
840 PRINT TAB(D1 + 6); "2) PRINT QUARTER'S SUMMARY"
850 PRINT TAB(D1 + 6); "3) PRINT YEAR'S SUMMARY"
970 IF A <4 THEN PS = A: GOSUB 6000
```

Lines 810 and 820 display a heading for the menu.

Lines 830 to 850 display the options the Operator can select.

Line 970 in the Payroll Program directed the program to one of several subroutines to process the option the Operator selected using an ON GOSUB Instruction. In this program, all of the reports are printed using the same subroutine, GOSUB 6000. To distinguish which report is to be printed, the value of the Operator's response is recorded in the Variable PS, PS=A. The program then proceeds to the subroutine that prints the summary.

Adjusting the Heading

The subheading can now be adjusted to print the period of the summary.

```
Step 9.    Type In and Press Enter:

7550 P$ = "": ON PS GOTO 7552,7554,7556
7552 A$ = "For Month Ending " + TD$: GOTO 7560
7554 A$ = "For Quarter Ending " + TD$: GOTO 7560
7556 A$ = "For Year Ending " + TD$
7560 TB = INT((110 - LEN(A$))/2): GOSUB 5990
7570 GOSUB 140: GOSUB 120: IF IN = 1 THE RETURN
```

Line 7550 uses the value recorded in the Variable PS to determine which heading to print.

Lines 7552 to 7556 record the heading to be used in the Variable A$.

Line 7560 calculates a tab setting for the Variable TB that centers the heading on the page. For this example, the width of the paper is 110 characters or 11 inches, with 10 characters per inch.

Line 7570 is used to print the heading.

Determining Beginning Dates for Summary

The data to be printed in the summary must be selected according to whether the summary is for the month, quarter, or year. This selection process is based on the premise that the summaries are printed on the last day of the month to record the transactions that have occurred up to that time. The program therefore uses the value of the month to determine what data to print.

Step 10. Type In and Press Enter:

```
510 PRINT TAB(D1 + 8);"PAYROLL SUMMARY PROGRAM"
520 PRINT TAB(D1 + 8);"------------------------"
550 MO = VAL(TD$):QU = INT((MO - 1)/3) * 3 + 1
```

Line 550 is added to the initial lines of the program right after the Operator enters the date into the Variable TD$. The value for the month can be determined using the VAL Instruction because the date is recorded as a number, "4-1-84". The VAL Instruction establishes the value based on the first numeric digits. As soon as a non-numeric digit, such as a hyphen, is encountered, the remainder of the String is ignored.

The calculation to determine the first month of the quarter, QU, is a little more complicated. The steps below describe the sequence this calculation follows.

1. The number of the quarter for any given month is determined by subtracting one from the month, dividing this by three, and finding the integer value of the result, INT((MO – 1)/3). The results of this calculation are shown below for each month of the year.

```
Month (MO):       1 2 3 4 5 6 7 8 9 10 11 12
INT((MO – 1)/3):  0 0 0 1 1 1 2 2 2 3  3  3
```

If a value of one were added to the above results, the number of the quarter for each month of the year would be established. However, for this calculation, the information required is the number of the first month for each quarter.

2. To determine the number of the first month for each quarter, the results from the calculation in Step 1, INT((MO – 1)/3), are multiplied by three. The results of these calculations are shown below for each month of the year.

```
Month:            1 2 3 4 5 6 7 8 9 10 11 12
INT((MO – 1)/3):  0 0 0 1 1 1 2 2 2 3  3  3
Times 3:          0 0 0 3 3 3 6 6 6 9  9  9
```

3. By adding a value of one to the results of the multiplication indicated above, INT((MO – 1)/3)*3, the number of the first month for each quarter is determined.

Selecting the Data

The data to be printed in the summary is determined from the values calculated in Step 10.

Step 11.   Type In and Press Enter:

```
6102 A = VAL(ED$(PP)):ON PS GOTO 6104,6106,6108
6104 IF A < MO THEN GOTO 6120
6106 IF A < QU THEN GOTO 6120
6108 IF A > MO OR GP(E,PP) = < 0 THEN GOTO 6120
```

    PS   Payroll Summary Period

Line 6102 determines the value for the ending date of the current Pay Period being processed, ED$(PP). This value is recorded in the Variable A. The program is then passed to the line which determines whether the information for the current Pay Period should be used. The specific line to be used is determined by the Variable PS, which records the period of the summary to be printed.

Line 6104 evaluates which ending dates are for the current month. If the value in the Variable A is less than the value for the current month, as recorded in the Variable MO, the program proceeds to the next Pay Period, GOTO 6120, without using the current data. This filters out the information that has been recorded for months prior to the current month.

Line 6106 determines if the data for the Pay Period is prior to the first month of the current quarter.

Line 6108 determines if the value of the current month is for a date later in the year. This allows the Payroll Summary Program to reprint information from previous summary periods. For example, the report for the month of February can be reprinted in June. To do this, the date the program is run is entered as 2-28-84. The program then retrieves all of the pay records for the year up to June, with Line 6104 bypassing the information for January and Line 6108 bypassing information for March through June. The result is a report that only prints the information from February.

Line 6108 also determines if any Gross Pay is indicated for the current month. The Gross Pay would be zero for Pay Periods prior to the time an employee is hired or after he or she leaves.

Totaling the Data

A standard routine totals the data for the summaries.

```
Step 12.  Type In and Press Enter:

        6065 RE = 0:OE = 0:GP = 0:FT = 0:SS = 0:ST = 0:SD = 0:NP = 0
        6112 RE = RE + RE(E,PP):OE = OE + OE(E,PP)
        6114 GP = GP + GP(E,PP):FT = FT + FT(E,PP):SS = SS + SS(E,PP)
        6116 ST = ST + ST(E,PP):SD = SD + SD(E,PP):NP = NP + NP(E,PP)
        6122 GOSUB 6800:REM  Print Totals
        6124 TR(E) = RE:TE(E) = OE:TG(E) = GP:TF(E) = FT
        6126 TS(E) = SS:TX(E) = ST:TD(E) = SD:TN(E) = NP
```

In the original summary routine, the totaling Variables were set to zero before the
FOR NEXT Loop for the employees was started.

Line 6065 clears the Variables used for totaling the information for each employee
before the next one is processed.

Lines 6112 to 6116 total the results from each Pay Period from the appropriate
Arrays.

Line 6122 directs the program to the subroutine that prints the totals at the bottom of
the summary for each employee.

Lines 6124 and 6126 record the totals for each employee in Arrays that are used to
summarize the information for all the employees.

Pause Control

A pause control is necessary if all the employees will not fit onto a single
sheet of paper.

```
Step 13.  Type In and Press Enter:

        6130 PRINT TAB(D1 + 6);"PUT IN A NEW SHEET OF PAPER"
        6140 PRINT TAB(D1 + 6);"TO CONTINUE PRESS (ENTER)";
        6150 INPUT A$:PL = 0
```

This is a standard pause control used after the data for each employee is printed.

The program can be modified for continuous-form paper by adding the following line
to the program. This eliminates the pause control.

```
Step 13.  Continuous Form.  Type In and Press Enter:

        6125 VT = 51 + VS:GOSUB 160:GOTO 6160
```

Line 6125 sets the vertical tab for paper that is 8-1/2-inches long (8.5 times 6 lines per
inch).

SUMMARY FOR ALL EMPLOYEES

The following summary combines the totals for each employee to establish a grand total for the entire work force. Essentially, the summary routine from the Payroll Program is used with a few slight modifications.

Summary Heading

The summary heading used for the Payroll Program can be used for this summary report. The only addition is a line specifying the period the report covers and the date the report is prepared.

```
Step 14.  Type In and Press Enter:

6550 P$ = "":ON PS GOTO 6552,6554,6556
6552 A$ = "For Month Ending " + TD$:GOTO 6560
6554 A$ = "For Quarter Ending " + TD$:GOTO 6560
6556 A$ = "For Year Ending " + TD$
```

Line 6550 selects the heading to be used based on the value stored in the Variable PS. Lines 6552 to 6556 establish the appropriate heading and combine it with the date.

Printing the Data

The routine used to build a line of data must be altered to retrieve the values from the new Arrays.

```
Step 15.  Type In and Press Enter:

6720 V = TR(E):TB = 35:GOSUB 5900:REM   Regular Earnings
6730 V = TE(E):TB = 45:GOSUB 5900:REM   Overtime Earnings
6740 V = TG(E):TB = 55:GOSUB 5900:REM   Gross Pay
6750 V = TF(E):TB = 65:GOSUB 5900:REM   FIT
6760 V = TS(E):TB = 75:GOSUB 5900:REM   FICA
6770 V = TX(E):TB = 85:GOSUB 5900:REM   SIT
6780 V = TD(E):TB = 95:GOSUB 5900:REM   SDI
6790 V = TN(E):TB = 105:GOSUB 5900:REM   Net Pay
```

Lines 6720 to 6790 already exist in the program, but the new Arrays must be used to determine the values for the Variable V.

Totaling the Data

The lines that total the data of individual employees are changed to the new Arrays.

Step 16. Type In and Press Enter:

```
6250 RESTORE
6300 IF TG(E) = <0 THEN GOTO 6360
6304 RE = RE + TR(E):OE = OE + TE(E):GP = GP + TG(E)
6306 FT = FT + TF(E):SS = SS + TS(E):ST = ST + TX(E)
6308 SD = SD + TD(E):NP = NP + TN(E)
```

Line 6250 occurs before the **FOR NEXT** Loop begins, ensuring that the program starts with the records of the first employee.

Line 6300 determines if there is any data for the current employee. If there is none, the program progresses to the next employee.

Lines 6304 to 6308 total the information.

Closing the Year

For systems with Disk Drives, the year can be closed by setting the record of the last Pay Period processed to zero. This causes the Pay Period to be set to one the next time the Payroll Program is run. This record is kept in the file named LASTPAY.

Step 17. Type In and Press Enter:

```
990 GOSUB 8200:PRINT:PRINT "THE END":END
8200 CLS: REM  Alternate:  8200 PRINT CHR$(12);
8205 IF MO <12 THEN RETURN
8210 PRINT TAB(D1 + 7);"PREPARE TO START NEW YEAR":PRINT
8220 PRINT TAB(D1 + 4);"IS THE DISK READY ( <Y> OR N)";
8230 A$ = "":INPUT A$:IF A$ = "N" OR A$ = "n" THEN RETURN
8240 PP$ = "0"
```

Line 990 is modified to direct the program to the subroutine starting at Line 8200 when the program is ended.

Line 8205 determines if the last month of the year has been reached. If it has not, this subroutine is terminated.

Line 8210 is the prompt that warns the Operator of the action to be taken.

Line 8240 sets the value recorded by this file to zero.

The actual storage routine is already a part of the program as Lines 8250 to 8280, see page 89.

Program Variations

The Payroll Program and Payroll Summary Program described in this book were designed as demonstrations to show how information flows through a computer. To include all of the routines required for any possible payroll configuration would require several volumes with annual updates. Moreover, the information and routines would be so extensive that only 10 percent of the information would be useful to any individual business.

While extensive listings of additional routines are beyond the scope of this book, this chapter does suggest variations to the programs for different payroll requirements. These suggestions analyze certain problems and show how changes in the existing programs would solve them. These examples can be used as an exercise in developing original routines for the demonstration programs before an attempt is made to develop completely original programs. They illustrate how changing a few lines in a program can produce strikingly different results.

Adding Fractions of Hours

The current entry routine allows full hours to be entered. Fractions of hours can be added manually by calculating the decimal equivalent of additional minutes before the hours are entered. Or, the program can be modified to ask for "Additional Minutes", which are then automatically converted to decimal values.

The following instructions show how to add minutes to the hourly total. First an INPUT Instruction is used to establish the number of minutes. After the minutes are entered, the program converts them to a decimal value and adds them to the total hours.

```
1052 PRINT "ADDITIONAL MINUTES";:INPUT A
1054 IF A>0 THEN W1(E)=W1(E)+A/60
```

These instructions occur after the hours are entered for week one. Similar instructions would have to be added after the INPUT Instruction for week two and after the INPUT Instructions in the correction routine. These INPUT Instructions may be found in Lines 1050, 1060, 3530, and 3550.

Additional Earnings

The current Payroll Program calculates an employee's earnings based solely on the number of hours worked. However, the employee's compensation might be increased by tips, commissions, bonuses, vacation pay, and/or sick pay. The government also requires that the value of goods for clothing, food, and lodging be taxed when they are offered in lieu of cash payments. Paychecks may also include a reimbursement for out-of-pocket expenses.

Two main factors must be considered when these additional earnings are added to the program: how frequently they will be paid and whether they are taxable or nontaxable.

Frequency of Payment

Bonuses are usually paid once a year. When this is the case, an INPUT Instruction for bonuses should not be included in the entry routine. This is because the Operator would have to respond to this question for every employee for every Pay Period though the bonus is issued only once a year. The INPUT Instruction for bonuses should therefore be added as an option within the correction routine, Lines 3500 to 3590, "Correct: 1=Week One 2=Week Two 3=Add Bonus?"

When employees receive bonuses and vacation pay, it might be a good idea to create a general classification, "Additional Earnings." For this classification, one INPUT Instruction would record the amount earned while the second INPUT Instruction would describe extra earnings, such as vacation or bonus pay. The description of the extra earnings should be printed on the Paycheck and in a special column for the summary of the current Pay Period. The description does not, however, need to be carried over for the Payroll Summary Program.

Tips for waitresses and waiters should be added for every Pay Period. In this case, the INPUT Instruction can be added as a part of the initial entry routine as well as the correction routine. Tips might require two separate INPUT Instructions and Arrays, one for "Tips Reported" and a second for "Tips Collected."

In the case of "Tips Reported", the employee simply reports to the employer the cash received directly from customers. This amount must be used in calculating Income Tax withholding, but the money never passes through the employer's hands. In other words, the value should be added to the Gross Pay before the withholding taxes are calculated and entered as a deduction before the Net Pay is established.

"Tips Collected" is used when the employer charges a gratuity for parties which is then distributed to the appropriate employees. The "Tips Collected" value must be added to the Gross Pay after the hourly wages are calculated and before the withholding deductions are determined. It remains a part of the Net Pay.

Nontaxable Reimbursements

Certain jobs require employees to buy supplies with their own money, for which they are later reimbursed. This reimbursement can be included in the Paycheck. A reimbursement for an expense in the line of work is not money the employee has earned. This money should therefore be added to the Gross Pay after the withholding taxes are calculated. A separate notation on the Paycheck and the Payroll Summary should describe this amount.

Recording Additional Deductions

Many different items are deducted from wages: charitable contributions, credit union deductions, dental plans, disability insurance, health plans, life insurance, loan repayments, union dues, etc. Some deductions may be made automatically each Pay Period, while others may be occasional deductions. An automatic deduction, such as union dues, may be a fixed amount, a percentage of the Gross Pay, or an amount based on the number of hours worked. If all employees are subject to exactly the same automatic deduction, the value can be written directly into the program. If the values vary from employee to employee but remain the same for an individual employee from Pay Period to Pay Period, the information can be added as another item in the DATA Instructions. Deductions which have no fixed pattern must be entered using INPUT Instructions.

When many special deductions are included, a separate Payroll Deduction Summary may need to be created. Additional reports can also be added to the Payroll Summary Program for reporting to unions, insurance companies, and banks handling savings plans.

Changing the Pay Period

The programs are currently designed for a biweekly Pay Period. The Tax Tables provide different tables for daily, weekly, semimonthly, monthly, quarterly, semiannually, and annually calculated Pay Periods.

The biweekly Pay Period was selected for this demonstration because it allows overtime pay to be automatically calculated by the program.

A semimonthly Pay Period produces Paychecks on a regular twice-a-month basis such as the first and fifteenth. When this is the case, the hours from fractions of a week must be considered and overtime cannot be automatically calculated.

To modify the programs for a semimonthly Pay Period, the following changes should be made to the program.

1. Change the INPUT Instructions for the hours from "Week One" and "Week Two" to "Regular Hours" and "Overtime Hours." The program already has Arrays assigned to record these hours which can be used with these INPUT Instructions.

2. Eliminate the instructions in the program used to calculate the number of regular and overtime hours. These calculations occur in Lines 4040 to 4070.

3. Change the Tax Tables from the biweekly schedule to the semimonthly schedule. This affects Lines 4200 to 4595.

Adding a Monthly Pay Period

A biweekly or semimonthly payroll is adequate when all employees are paid by the number of hours worked. But management personnel are usually paid a fixed monthly salary.

The following steps allow the program to be used for both types of payroll.

1. Expand the Employee Code so a value of one indicates employees paid by the hour and a value of two indicates employees paid a monthly salary.

The rate of pay stored in the Variable P can be used for both hourly wages and monthly salaries because the value of the Employee Code stored in the Variable C will determine how this value is used.

2. Bypass the INPUT routine for number of hours worked for salaried employees. Determine the Gross Pay directly from the rate of pay stored in the Variable P. The following lines alter this routine.

```
1030 ON C+1 GOTO 1400,1035,1200
1110 GOTO 1400
1200 REM  Salaried Employees
1220 GP(E)=P
1400 NEXT N
```

Line 1030 uses the value of the Employee Code to select the appropriate portion of the program. If the code is for a former employee, C=0, the program progresses to the next employee, GOTO 1400. If the employee is an hourly worker, the program passes to Line 1035, which is the beginning of the INPUT routine for the number of hours worked. If an employee is salaried, C=2, the program passes to Line 1200.

Line 1220 transfers the salary from the rate-of-pay Variable to the Gross Pay Array.

3. Establish a new set of Tax Tables for the monthly payroll. The following lines access these tables from the initial entry routine.

```
1230 GOSUB 14000
14000 REM  Monthly Tax Tables
14695 RETURN
```

The program lines for calculating FIT, FICA, SIT, SDI, and Net Pay for the monthly payroll follow the same structure as the lines used for the biweekly payroll described on pages 96 to 107.

4. Add an initial menu to the program to determine which payroll is to be processed. The options include: "1) Hourly Only," "2) Salaried Only," and "3) Hourly & Salaried." Record the value from this menu in the Variable PY which is used in the entry routine as indicated below.

```
1035 IF PY = 2 THEN GOTO 1400
1210 IF PY = 1 THEN GOTO 1400
```

Line 1035 occurs before any hourly employee is processed. If only salaried employees are being paid, PY=2, the program is directed to the next employee.

Line 1210 occurs before any of the salaried employees are processed. If only hourly employees are being paid, PY=1, the program is directed to the next employee.

5. Extend the Payroll Summary Program to accept the additional Pay Periods generated when only salaried employees are being paid. This change must be made to Lines 610 to 630.

Printing W-2 Forms

The W-2 Form is issued at the end of the year by the employer. Copies are given to the employee and the government. The structure of the printing routine follows the principles described for the Record of an Individual Transaction. Therefore, the routine for the Paycheck from the Payroll Program can be modified and added to the Payroll Summary Program to print W-2 forms.

The federal government provides W-2 Forms with three forms per page, see Appendix B. If this type of form is used, the program needs to be modified so that the print routine processes three employees automatically but then pauses and informs the Operator to insert a new page before the next three employee forms are printed.

To do this, the routine for continuous forms described on page 133 needs to precede the pause control for changing the page described on page 134. A special counter can be maintained in the Variable PF to record the number of forms that have been printed. When less than three forms have been printed, the continuous forms routine can be used. As soon as the third form on the page is printed, the value of the Variable PF should be set to zero and the program directed to the pause control.

Storing Employee Records on Disk

The employee records are currently stored as a part of the program in DATA Instructions. They are retrieved using the READ Instruction. This is the easiest and fastest method. It is appropriate when the turnover rate is low and wages are only changed once or twice a year and is a viable approach so long as the person who maintains the payroll records knows how to modify the programs.

However, if the employee status changes frequently or the person in charge of the payroll does not know programming, the employee records should be maintained as a Disk file. This allows the records to be changed by responding to prompts similar to the ones used to enter the employee hours.

The following description outlines how a separate program can be developed to maintain the employee records. The routines for this program follow the same structure as the Payroll Program.

1. Start the program with a retrieval routine that records the data about the employees in a series of Arrays. The basic structure for a retrieval routine is described on pages 87 and 88. The following factors must also be considered.

a. An initial line should direct the program to the retrieval routine.

b. The retrieval routine should start with an Input Instruction that establishes the number of employees to be retrieved. This value can be stored in the Variable W which is used by the current programs for this information.

c. If more than ten employees are to be recorded, an initial DIM Instruction should be used to establish the number of employees to be processed.

Indicated below is an example of the lines used to perform these functions.

```
600 GOSUB 9600
9670 INPUT#1,W
9672 WT = W + 3
9674 DIM E(WT),N$(WT),F$(WT),P(WT)
9676 DIM M(WT),X(WT),C(WT),S$(WT)
```

Line 600 directs the program to the retrieval routine as soon as the program begins.

Line 9670 is the INPUT Instruction which retrieves the number of employees currently recorded.

Line 9672 establishes the maximum number of employees to be processed at a value that is three times larger than the current number of employees. This allows new employees to be added.

Lines 9674 to 9676 set the dimension of the Arrays for the employee records.

2. Establish an initial menu to indicate the functions that can be performed with the employee records. Some suggested options are indicated below.

1. Add a New Employee
2. Display Current Employees
3. Change an Employee's File
8. Store the Employee Records
11. End the Program

The numbers of the options included here are consistent with the numbers of the options used by the Payroll Program. For example, Option 8 is the storage function in both programs.

3. The routine for adding a new employee can simply be a sequence of INPUT Instructions that requests the appropriate information for each of the employee Arrays.

After adding the employee, increase the total number of employees stored in the Variable W by a value of one.

Use an initial line at the beginning of this routine to establish when the maximum number of employees has been reached. The maximum value is recorded in the Variable WT, so when the value of the Variable W equals the value of the Variable WT, W=WT, no more employees may be added. A message should inform the Operator that the program can accept no more employees at the current time. Additional employees can be added simply by running the program a second time because the Arrays are dimensioned by Step 1 to include three employees more than the current work force.

4. Display the information about the current employees using the existing routine in the Payroll Program, Lines 2500 to 2650.

5. Add a correction routine to change the information about any employee. First, display the list of employees. Then use an INPUT Instruction to select the employee to be changed. Next, display the data about the employee in a numbered list as indicated below. Any item in this list can be changed by entering the number of the item. Then use this number in an ON GOTO Instruction to direct the program to an INPUT Instruction that will change the appropriate Array.

1. Last Name: Harrison
2. First Name: James
3. Rate of Pay: 5.25
4. Marital Status: 1
5. Tax Exemptions: 1
6. Employee Code: 1
7. Social Security #: 534-65-1032

6. The storage routine follows the same pattern of instructions as the retrieval routine. Simply delete the DIM Instruction indicated in Step 1.

7. Add the retrieval routine from this program to the Payroll Program and the Payroll Summary Program to replace the current DATA Instructions. Make the following changes.

a. The initial line that previously established the number of employees should direct the program to the new retrieval routine. This line is indicated below.

```
600 GOSUB 9600:REM  Retrieve Employee Records
```

b. Replace the READ Instruction in Line 9500 with lines that transfer information from the employee Arrays to the employee Variables.

```
9500 E = N:REM   Retrieve Employee Record
9502 N$ = N$(E):F$ = F$(E):P = P(E)
9504 M = M(E):X = X(E):C = C(E):S$ = S$(E)
```

Line 9500 sets the value of the Variable E to the value of the Variable N. The Variable E records the Employee Number. It is set to the same value as the counter for the FOR NEXT Loop, the Variable N, to match the Employee Records with the Arrays used to record earnings and deductions.

Year-to-Date

An additional modification to the program can be used to store an additional year-to-date figure for the Gross Pay. The value of the year-to-date amount can then be used to determine when the limits for the Social Security and State Disability withholdings have been reached.

The following modifications are required to add the year-to-date amount.

a. Include an Input Instruction for the year-to-date figure, INPUT#1,YD(N), in the retrieval routine.

b. Modify the calculation routines for FICA and SDI by deleting the questions for the Operator and replacing them with an IF THEN Instruction. The instruction for the FICA calculation is indicated below.

```
4110 IF YD(E)>37800 THEN GOTO 4200
```

c. Add the routine for storing the employee records to the Payroll Program. Access this routine after the payroll data is stored so that the employee records will be updated with the latest year-to-date information. The year-to-date data stored by this routine should be a combination of the current year-to-date value plus the Gross Pay value: PRINT#1,YD(N)+GP(N).

CREATING ORIGINAL PROGRAMS

This book shows how information processed by manual systems can be converted for automated processing by a computer. The previous section of the book used the specific example of the Payroll Program to illustrate the conversion process. This section provides a series of questions that can be used to evaluate whether a given job should be converted into a program. It then outlines a procedure that can be used as a guide for creating original programs.

Three basic steps must be performed to convert a manual system to an automated one: the task to be performed must be evaluated; program routines for each function must be created; the completed routines must be tested.

Evaluating the Task

The key to converting a task from a manual to an automated system is to first identify the patterns used to process the information in the manual system. This is necessary because computers follow instructions on a repeat basis. Therefore, there must be some pattern to the way the information is handled. A careful analysis of the existing patterns and forms used to complete a task manually can dictate the bulk of the design of a computer program.

Creating Program Routines

After establishing the patterns of information flow, the task should be divided into manageable functions. Separate functions should be identified for input, manipulation, and output of the data. The functions can then be broken down into subfunctions until individual working units are established.

These working units can then be translated into patterns of program instructions a computer can follow. Many of these working units can be created using the structures of program lines described in this section. This is possible because the computer must follow standard procedures to accomplish basic functions. Since the structure of the procedure dictates the sequence of lines, the process of designing the routines is simply a matter of adapting the program lines to the specific information required.

For example, in the payroll programs described in this book, a standard display routine was used four different times. The print routine for the summary reports was used three times. And the menu and retrieval routines were used in both the Payroll Program and the Payroll Summary Program with only slight variations.

The bulk of most programs can therefore be created by identifying standard functions and using the structures of program lines described in this section. This allows the programmer to devote most of his or her efforts to the unique requirements of the task to be performed.

Testing the Program

Each working unit should be tested as soon as it is completed to ensure that it is operating properly. Additional tests should be performed to ensure that new working units function properly in relation to the rest of the program.

Should the Task be Computerized?

Determining whether a specific information processing task is appropriate for a computer requires an analysis of the job to be performed. The following questions can be used as a part of this evaluation procedure.

How often will the program be used? It will take at least four to six times as long to create a program to perform a task as it takes to perform the task manually. If a job is to be performed only once a year, there may be no reason for using a computer to do the task.

Does the information being processed follow a pattern? A computer program is a series of instructions that follows the pattern of the task to be performed. If the work being done does not follow a pattern, the instructions cannot be organized into a program. For example, when an original oil painting is created, the subject, colors, size of canvas, and direction of brush strokes are unique to the specific work being developed. On the other hand, in musical notation, the staff, clef signatures, shape of the notes, and position of the notes on the staff follow regular patterns. The process of creating an oil painting would therefore be difficult to computerize, while the process of recording a musical score is a viable possiblity.

Can the information be entered into the computer initially? If the information to be processed must first be handwritten or typed and then entered into the computer at a later time, the efficiency of the system is greatly reduced. For example, when checks are written from a personal checking account, the transaction may take place in a variety of locations. If the computer is subsequently used to record these transactions, all of the information must be entered a second time into the computer. The resulting record may be neater than the information contained on the check stub, but the amount of time required to perform the task is twice as long as necessary.

How complicated is the job? The more complicated a job, the more likely the computer will be able to save time and effort. The computer can follow a vast array of instructions and perform complicated calculations almost instantaneously. For example, to determine the postage to ship a book overseas by air requires four separate calculations that vary according to the specific destination. The charge for the package is one rate for the first ounce, a second rate for the next three ounces, a third rate for every additional two ounces up to 32 ounces, and a fourth rate for every eight ounces over 32 ounces. The calculation becomes more complicated because most scales record weight as pounds and ounces, so the weight of the parcel in pounds must be converted to ounces before the appropriate weight can be determined. This is an involved calculation when performed manually, but the computer can do it effortlessly.

How frequently is a task repeated? It takes a certain amount of time to turn on a computer, select a program, and initiate its operation. If several transactions can be processed at a time instead of just one, the savings in time and effort is greatly increased. For example, a business using a manual bookkeeping system will usually write up its invoices every day, even if there are only two or three, so that the work load does not get backed up. A business using a computerized bookkeeping system may process all of its invoices once each week, recording 20 to 50 transactions in the same time four or five invoices can be created by hand.

How many different ways will the information be used? A computer program can take the information from a single input and automatically produce several different outputs in a variety of formats. For example, when a sales transaction is recorded, the name of the customer can be used to create an invoice, shipping label, sales ledger entry, and statements as well as mailing labels for subsequent advertising. The effort of typing the name once is thus automatically leveraged into multiple uses.

Will the information be correlated with data from other programs? Computer programs invariably record the information they generate in some machine-readable form the computer can access at a later time. This means the information from one program can automatically be transferred to a different program, eliminating the need for manual reentry of the data by the Operator. For example, a sales transaction can be recorded as it occurs. This can then be retrieved by a different program at the end of a day to generate a sales summary. The sales summary can then be retrieved at the end of the month for a profit and loss statement. In the meantime, an inventory program can access the same data to adjust the records of the stock on hand. The information from the inventory program can then be used by a purchasing program to replenish the depleted stock. This automatic transfer of information from one use to another increases the efficiency of the overall system.

If a task to be computerized does not meet at least one of these criteria, perhaps the information should be processed manually rather than by a computer.

Describe the Job

The task the computer is to perform should be carefully defined. This should start with a short general description that indicates the purpose of the program. The task can then be broken down into functions which indicate the initial information that is required, data to be entered from the Keyboard, manipulations the program is to perform, and the output that will be required. Throughout this process, any forms available from manual systems should be used as guides.

The outline on page 166 gives an overview of the factors that need to be considered as the program is developed. These factors are described in more detail in the comments below.

General Description

First, establish a general description that gives an overview of the function the program is to perform.

Limit the scope of the program description to a single task, if possible. For example, the scope of the program should not be "to perform all bookkeeping chores" because this includes many separate tasks such as accounts payable, accounts receivable, payroll, inventory control, etc.

It is better to have individual programs perform single tasks. The results of these programs can then be correlated using summary programs. To determine the scope of an individual program, imagine describing the task to an intelligent but inexperienced worker. For example, to say to this person, "Take care of my bookkeeping," would be unreasonable. But to say, "This is how the payroll is processed," is manageable.

Forms from Manual Systems

If a task is important enough to be computerized, a parallel manual system is likely to be in operation. The procedures and forms used in these manual systems have probably been developed over a period of time, and they can represent a significant amount of thought and experience from people who have performed the task before. As such, these forms and procedures represent important research tools that can be used as guides during the design process.

An Outline for the Program Description

General Description
    Purpose of the Program
    Forms from the Manual System

Initial Information
    Establish Information from Forms
    Determine How Information is to be Stored
        Information as a Part of the Program
        Information in Multiple DATA Instructions
        Information Retrieved from the Storage Device

Information from the Keyboard
    Information Entry
    Corrections

Program Manipulations

Program Output
    To the Video Screen
    To the Printer
        Records of Individual Transactions
        Summary of Transactions
    To the Storage Device

Use the forms from manual systems to develop lists of the information they contain. Some items on these forms may be unnecessary, while other items of information may need to be added. But the forms should act as a foundation for designing the program.

Initial Information

A certain amount of information remains the same from one run of a program to the next. Identify this type of information by carefully reviewing the lists of information created from the forms. For example, if a program is being created for a business and the name of the business is to appear on the form, this information will not change.

Identify and classify information that will be used more than once into tables. Create separate tables for different types of information and make notations about how frequently the information will change.

Based on this frequency, make plans for how information should be stored. Information that is going to change once a year or less can be written directly into the program. Information that may change three or four times a year can be stored on Disk or Cassette Tape.

Information written directly into the program can be stored much more efficiently than information stored on Disk. For example, for the Payroll Program, ten lines of program were required to introduce the employee records using DATA Instructions. If this same information were stored and retrieved from Disk, a separate program to record and modify this information would require approximately 100 program lines. Similarly, information can be retrieved from DATA Instructions much faster than from Disk.

However, if the same information will be changed frequently or several programs are going to work from the same records, it is more convenient to record the data on Disk.

Fortunately, the programs can be changed from one option to the other with minimum effort. If day-to-day operations show one approach to be inefficient, the other option can be implemented.

Information from the Keyboard

Some information will change every time the program is used. This type of information is entered at the Keyboard.

The sequence in which this information is to be entered must be planned carefully to minimize the time and effort required by the Operator. Information that needs to be entered for every transaction and every run of the program should be requested automatically by the program. To pass from one item to the next, the Operator should only have to press the Enter Key. Information that is going to be requested occasionally, such as Christmas bonuses, can be entered through the correction routine. This allows the Operator to ignore the option for most runs of the program, yet use it when necessary.

Draw up two lists for the information to be entered. One list should indicate the data to be entered for every run. The second list should indicate information to be entered occasionally.

The Operator also must be given convenient options for correcting errors.

Program Manipulations

Manipulations and calculations are the heart of a computer program. If no manipulations need to be performed to the entered information, there is probably no need for a program. The calculations may be as simple as totaling multiple transactions. Or, the program may perform very complex computations.

To determine the exact sequence of manipulations and calculations to be made, process the task manually from beginning to end. List each of the required manipulations and calculations.

Program Output

If manipulations are the heart of a program, output is the reason for its existence. For example, it is possible to ask the computer to perform the following mathematical computation: $A=INT(100*(3-15)/(6+25))$.

The computer performs the task, but what difference does it make? The value of the computer is not realized until an output is generated: PRINT A.

The output of the program can be directed to the Video Screen, a printer, and/or a Disk or Cassette Tape. As before, the information and format for the output can be determined directly from the forms used for manual systems. More than likely, the output has been generated to complete one or more of these forms. If the information to be produced does not appear on an existing form, an original form can be created.

It is also possible that the output to the Disk or Cassette Tape will become the input for another program. If this is the case, the other programs in the system should be defined before any one program is created. In the process of defining the other programs, another item of data may be required and/or another manipulation to the data may need to be added.

Program Segments

Programs should be divided into separate functions, which should be clearly visible when the programs are listed. To do this, each function within a program should be assigned a block of lines. A consistent approach to these lines should be used so that routines from one program can easily be transferred to a different program.

Below is a suggested outline of the program Line Numbers and their respective functions.

Line Numbers	Function
0-799	Initial Controls
800-999	Main Menu
1000-1999	Entry Routines
2000-2999	Display Routines
3000-3999	Correction Routines
4000-4999	Calculations & Manipulations
5000-5999	Print Individual Records
6000-6999	Print Summaries
7000-7999	Miscellaneous Routines
8000-8999	Storage Routines
9000-9999	Retrieval Routines

The chapters that follow show how the information from the description can be converted into program routines.

Initial Information

Information that remains the same from one run of the program to the
next can be entered in one of three ways. The information can be written directly into
the program lines. READ and DATA Instructions can be used to record the data. Or
the information can be stored on Disk or Cassette Tapes and retrieved when the
program is first run.

Information in Program Lines

Certain information can be written directly into the program lines. This
information can be very specific, such as the name of an individual or a company
appearing in the heading of a form. Or, the information can be general, as represented
by the headings "Payroll Summary" and "Employee Records."

The contents and placement of this information usually evolve quite naturally as the
program is developed and do not need to be preplanned. The information will either be
a part of a PRINT Instruction or will be stored in a Variable for output to the printer.

READ/DATA Instructions

READ and DATA Instructions introduce information into a program
quickly and concisely. This approach is usually most appropriate when data from a
table, such as the employee records, needs to be introduced.

READ/DATA Instructions should be used when all or most of the data is to be used
in a sequential fashion. This is because the READ Instruction must start at the
beginning and proceed towards the end until the desired information is encountered.
For example, in the Payroll Program, these instructions were used to process all the
employees in the file.

It is not appropriate to use READ/DATA Instructions when the program must jump
to a specific piece of information. For example, the Tax Tables in the Payroll Program
were written directly into the program lines rather than entered in DATA Instructions.
This is because withholding for a married employee requires a different Tax Table from
that of a single person. If DATA Instructions were used, all of the information
from the single Tax Table would have to be read before the married Tax Table could be
used.

The following steps show how to prepare information for DATA Instructions. Two structures are suggested for the program lines. The first shows how information for a single table can be prepared. The second shows how more than one table can be used.

Single Data Table

The following steps indicate a structure for the program lines that follows the same concepts described for the Payroll Program.

1. A table can be created to indicate the sequence and format for the information following the example shown below.

```
           SAMPLE  TABLE  FOR  DATA

     #  |      Item 1      Item 2      Item 3
     1  |       1.1         1.2         1.3
     2  |       2.1         2.2         2.3
     3  |       3.1         3.2         3.3
```

2. The table can be converted into DATA lines using the following sequence.

To Enter Single Data Table:

```
9600 REM  Item 1, Item 2, Item 3
9610 DATA 1.1, 1.2, 1.3
9620 DATA 2.1, 2.2, 2.3
9630 DATA 3.1, 3.2, 3.3
```

3. Using a READ Instruction, the information can be recovered from the DATA Instructions.

To Retrieve Single Data Table:

```
2500 RESTORE
2510 FOR N = 1 TO T1
2570 GOSUB 9500:REM  Retrieve Information from DATA Lines
2590 PRINT R1,R2,R3
2600 NEXT N
2610 RETURN
9500 READ R1, R2, R3
9510 RETURN
```

Multiple Data Tables

More than one table can be stored in DATA Instructions. A title for each table should be recorded in an initial DATA Instruction. Then, when the information from this table is required, a READ Instruction retrieves all the DATA information until the title of the table appears.

1. A table can be created to indicate the sequence and format for the information following the example shown below.

SAMPLE TABLE FOR DATA (II)

#	Item A	Item B	Item C	Item D
1	1A	1B	1C	1D
2	2A	2B	2C	2D
3	3A	3B	3C	3D

2. The DATA Instructions that store this information are indicated below.

To Enter Multiple Data Tables:

```
9800 REM  Item A, Item B, Item C, Item D
9805 DATA Table #2, 3 Data Lines
9810 DATA 1A, 1B, 1C, 1D
9820 DATA 2A, 2B, 2C, 2D
9830 DATA 3A, 3B, 3C, 3D
```

Line 9805 is the DATA Instruction that identifies the beginning of the second table for the READ Instruction. This line includes one data item that is the title of the table and a second that indicates the length of the table.

3. The following lines show how to retrieve the second table.

```
                To Retrieve Multiple Data Tables:

2200 RESTORE
2202 READ A$:IF A$<>"Table #2" THEN GOTO 2202
2204 READ A$:T2=VAL(A$)
2210 FOR N=1 TO T2
2220 GOSUB 9700:REM  Retrieve Information from Table #2
2230 PRINT RA$, RB$, RC$, RD$
2300 NEXT N
2310 RETURN
9700 READ RA$,RB$,RC$,RD$
9710 RETURN
```

Line 2202 uses the READ Instruction to retrieve the information from the DATA Instructions until the identifying "Table #2" label is encountered.

Line 2204 illustrates how the number of DATA Instructions to be processed can be stored as a DATA value. In this example, Line 2204 reads the second value stored in Line 9805, "3 Lines of Data," and converts it to a value that can be used in the FOR NEXT Loop that follows. The value is stored in the Variable T2.

Information from Disk or Cassette Tapes

Initial information can be stored on Disk or Cassette Tapes. When this is done, the program should be directed to the appropriate retrieval subroutine(s) in the initial lines of the program.

This is the approach used in a Summary Program to retrieve the information stored by a Transaction Program. It can also be used to retrieve information that would otherwise be stored in DATA Instructions. However, when this is done, a separate program must be developed to store the initial records.

The example below shows the type of line that needs to be added to direct the program to a retrieval routine from the initial lines of the program. The structure of the retrieval routine is described later, see pages 186 and 187.

```
                To Retrieve Disk or Cassette Tape File:

700 GOSUB 9600:  REM  Retrieve Initial Record
```

Information from the Keyboard

Information that varies from one run of a program to the next is entered using INPUT Instructions. This information is stored in either Variables or Arrays.

When a single piece of information is to be entered, such as the date the program is run, the information can be stored in a Variable. The name of this Variable should be recorded so that it is not used for other purposes. If the same Variable is used in a second INPUT Instruction or appears on the left side of an equation, A$="No", the value currently in the Variable will be replaced by the new value.

When INPUT Instructions are used to record information for multiple transactions and/or calculations, an Array should be used to record the data. The Array allows different items of information to be processed through the same sequence of calculations and/or manipulations. The action to be performed is established by using the Array name. The information to be processed at any given time is controlled by the numeric value between the parentheses of the Array name. For example, Gross Pay can be determined by the formula GP(N)=HR(N)*P(N). The hours for each employee, HR(N), are all multiplied by the rate of pay, P(N). That is the fixed part of the formula. The actual employee being processed at any given time is determined by the value of the Variable N.

When an INPUT Instruction is used, it should always be preceded by a PRINT Instruction that identifies the information to be entered.

Identifying the Program Run

Most programs will need some form of information that identifies individual program runs. This information can be as simple as a date or it may require additional data.

This initial information should be carefully evaluated so that only essential data is required. It is easy to require the Operator to provide a long string of information. For example, the program might request the date, Operator's name, time the program is being run, supervisor who is verifying the information being processed, clerk who accumulated the data being entered, etc. In a large organization, this type of information might be useful for establishing responsibility for the data created. But for a small one-person firm, this information is useless.

The following example of an initial display identifies the program being run and uses an INPUT Instruction to establish the date.

```
To Enter Initial Program Information:

280 D1 = 20: REM  For 80 – Column Displays
282 REM  280 D1 = 0: REM  For 40 Column Displays
290 D3 = 24: D3 = D3 – 5: REM  Number of Lines on the Display
500 CLS: REM  Alternate:  500 PRINT CHR$(12);
510 PRINT TAB(D1 + 14); "PROGRAM NAME"
520 PRINT TAB(D1 + 14); "------------"
530 PRINT TAB(D1); "ENTER DATE MM – DD – YY (Jan 10: 1 – 10 – 84)"
540 PRINT "TODAY'S DATE"; : INPUT TD$
```

Entering Data

The information to be entered must be determined next. The information for the Payroll Program was easy to establish: it was the number of hours each employee worked per week. More information may be required for other programs.

Again, the best way to determine what information needs to be entered is to evaluate the forms used for manual systems. In the case of the Payroll Program, the form that establishes the information to be entered is the Time Card. For other programs, the information might come from a sales receipt, purchase order, request for quotation, or questionnaire. The forms the program will produce should also be examined as they may indicate additional information that must be entered, such as an address or telephone number.

Create a table that lists the information to be entered. This table should indicate the Array that is to record the data.

```
               INFORMATION TO BE ENTERED

        Information                      Array
        First Name                       N1$( )
        Second Name                      N2$( )
        First Value                      V1( )
        Second Value                     V2( )
```

Number of Transactions

If the program requires entering information for more than ten transactions, the maximum number of transactions to be processed must be established. This is because an Array can accept up to ten values, but if an attempt is made to use more than this, an error message is generated. However, DIM Instructions can be used to increase the maximum number of Variables an Array can access during the run of the program.

The following example prepares the DIM Instruction for the information indicated in the table above.

To Prepare Arrays:

```
650 TT = 50: REM  Maximum Number of Transactions
660 DIM N1$(TT),N2$(TT)
670 DIM V1(TT),V2(TT)
```

Processing Transactions

The body of the entry routine can now be established. This routine can be structured by placing a FOR NEXT Loop around all of the INPUT Instructions used to enter information in Arrays. The INPUT Instruction establishes the information to be entered, and the FOR NEXT Loop allows multiple transactions to be processed.

An example of the structure of INPUT Instructions is shown below. The information from the table on page 174 is used in this example.

To Enter Information:

```
710 GOSUB 1000:REM  Enter Data
990 END
1000 CLS: REM  Alternate:  1000 PRINT CHR$(12);
1010 FOR X = 1 TO TT
1100 PRINT "FIRST NAME";:INPUT N1$(X)
1110 PRINT "SECOND NAME";:INPUT N2$(X)
1200 PRINT "FIRST VALUE";:INPUT V1(X)
1210 PRINT "SECOND VALUE";:INPUT V2(X)
1400 NEXT X
1420 RETURN
```

Variable Number of Transactions

The routine above is appropriate when an identical number of transactions is processed each time the program is run. This is the case for the Payroll Program because each employee has to be processed. In other situations, the number of transactions will vary. For example, in a sales situation, 50 invoices might be processed during one run of the program and five the next. When this is the case, the Operator must be able to indicate that no more transactions are to be performed.

The control for ending an entry routine should occur as a result of the first INPUT Instruction inside the FOR NEXT Loop. The end control should be a value that would never need to be entered as a normal item of data. For example, if a String Array is used in the first INPUT Instruction, the end control might be the word "end". If the first INPUT Instruction is for a numeric value, the end control could be either no value or a negative value. If the INPUT Instruction must be able to accept any numeric value, the response can be entered using a String Variable. When this is the case, the word "end" can be used to terminate the routine. If the routine is not terminated, the value in the String Variable can be converted to a numeric value using the VAL Instruction, and the rest of the INPUT Instructions can then be processed.

The following lines add the "end" control to the existing entry routine.

```
                 To Terminate Entry Routine:

    1015 PRINT TAB(D1);"TO END ROUTINE TYPE: END(ENTER)"
    1105 IF N1$(X) = "END" OR N1$(X) = "end" THEN GOTO 1440
    1410 PRINT TAB(D1 + 6);"NO MORE DATA CAN BE ENTERED"
    1420 PRINT TAB(D1 + 6);"TO CONTINUE PRESS (ENTER)";
    1430 INPUT A$
    1440 LX = X - 1:IF X = <TT THEN N1$(X) = ""
    1450 RETURN
```

Line 1005 informs the Operator how to terminate the entry routine.

Line 1105 determines if the "end" control has been used. If it has, the program proceeds to Line 1440.

Lines 1410 to 1430 are a pause control that occur at the end of the FOR NEXT Loop. They inform the Operator that no more information can be entered.

Line 1440 establishes the number of transactions processed in the Variable LX. If the last transaction processed occurs before the end of the FOR NEXT Loop, X=<TT, the "end" control is erased from the last Variable of the Array.

The information entry routine should be a subroutine so the RETURN Instruction in Line 1450 terminates it.

Using Stored Data for Input

The Payroll Program combined information from the INPUT Instructions with information from DATA Instructions by simply processing the data in the same sequence for each run. Other programs will need to correlate stored information with input information in a less structured fashion. For example, the stored information might be a list of regular customers. In this case, the information for a given customer would not be needed for every run of the program.

The program requires a process that allows the Operator to specify the data to be used. When the information is found, it can be transferred to the Array for the current transaction. The following program lines show how to merge information using this approach.

To Select Stored Information:

```
1020 PRINT "ENTER CUSTOMER NUMBER";:INPUT A$
1025 IF A$ = "END" OR A$ = "end" THEN GOTO 1440
1030 IF A$ = "" THEN GOTO 1100
1040 RESTORE
1050 READ N$:IF N$ = A$ THEN GOTO 1090
1060 IF N$ <> "THE END" THEN GOTO 1050
1070 PRINT TAB(D1 + 7);"THAT NUMBER IS NOT ON FILE"
1080 GOTO 1020
1090 READ N1$(X),N2$(X):GOTO 1200
9990 DATA THE END
```

Line 1020 determines the customer's number.

Line 1030 determines when no number is entered. It directs the program to the routine that uses the INPUT Instruction to enter the information about the customer.

Line 1050 searches for the number in the DATA file. If the number is located, it directs the program to Line 1090.

Lines 1060 to 1080 search through to the end of the data information until the number is found. If the number is not found, Line 1070 informs the Operator.

Line 1090 transfers the information from the customer file to the Array for the transaction. It then directs the program to the routine that establishes the values for the current transaction, GOTO 1200.

Line 9990 is added as the last DATA Instruction. If this control is not used, an error message will occur after the READ Instruction reaches the last item in the DATA Instructions.

Correlating Arrays with Input Data

Fixed information retrieved from Disk or Cassette Tape and stored in Arrays is always available to the program. To use this information, it is only necessary to record a number that establishes the position of the information in the Array. This approach can be used to record inventory items. For example, an inventory item can be identified by a name, abbreviation, price, and weight. When a sale is recorded, the number of the item can be used to refer to all of this data. In the demonstration program, assume the value stored in the Array $V1(\ )$ refers to an inventory number. The name of the item could be printed on an invoice by using $IT\$(V1(X))$. The following is a breakdown of how a program records the information.

X	Number of the Transaction
V1( )	Number of the Inventory Item
IT$( )	Name of the Inventoried Item

Correcting Information

During an entry routine, the program should proceed automatically from one item to the next. For a correction routine, the Operator must be allowed to pick out an individual item to correct without having to process the other items. The following steps are required to accomplish this.

1. Display all items that require INPUT Instructions in a numbered list.

2. The Operator can then select the number of the item to be changed. If the Operator wishes to discontinue the corrections, the Enter Key can be pressed without entering a number.

3. The number the Operator selects directs the program to an INPUT Instruction for the information to be changed.

4. After the Operator enters a new value, the numbered list is redisplayed to include the new value of the changed item.

5. The Operator is once again given the option to select an item to be changed or to discontinue the correction routine.

The following routine shows how this function can be structured.

```
                    To Correct Entered Information:

          1300 PRINT:PRINT "CORRECT THIS DATA (Y OR <N>)";
          1310 A$ = "":INPUT A$:A = 2:IF A$ = "Y" OR A$ = "y" THEN A = 1
          1320 IF A = 1 THEN GOSUB 3500
          3500 CLS: REM  Alternate:  3500 PRINT CHR$(12);
          3510 PRINT "1) FIRST NAME ";N1$(X)
          3520 PRINT "2) SECOND NAME ";N2$(X)
          3530 PRINT "3) FIRST VALUE";V1(X)
          3540 PRINT "4) SECOND VALUE";V2(X)
          3550 PRINT:PRINT "TO DISCONTINUE PRESS (ENTER)"
          3560 PRINT "SELECT NUMBER OF ITEM TO CORRECT";
          3570 A$ = "":INPUT A$:IF A$ = "" THEN RETURN
          3580 PRINT:A = VAL(A$):ON A GOTO 3610, 3620, 3630, 3640
          3590 GOTO 3500
          3610 PRINT "FIRST NAME";:INPUT N1$(X):GOTO 3500
          3620 PRINT "SECOND NAME";:INPUT N2$(X):GOTO 3500
          3630 PRINT "FIRST VALUE";:INPUT V1(X):GOTO 3500
          3640 PRINT "SECOND VALUE";:INPUT V2(X):GOTO 3500
```

Lines 1300 to 1320 give the Operator the option to correct the information before the next transaction is processed.

Lines 3500 to 3570 display a numbered list of the information that can be changed.

Line 3550 informs the Operator that the correction routine can be discontinued by pressing the Enter Key.

Line 3580 uses the Operator's response to direct the program to the item to be changed.

Lines 3610 to 3640 are used to enter the new value. After each INPUT Instruction, a GOTO Instruction directs the program to the beginning of the correction display.

Program Manipulations

The manipulation phase of program development probably requires the greatest amount of planning and thought because there is no structured pattern that can be used as a guide. The manipulations and calculations must be tailored to the specific requirements of the job to be performed.

While there is no predetermined structure for the manipulation portion of the program, the following steps can be used as a guide for developing the necessary routines.

1. List the Calculations to be Performed.
2. Write Descriptions for Each Calculation.
3. Translate the Descriptions into Program Lines.
4. Test the Calculation Routines.
5. Direct the Program to the Calculations.

List the Manipulations & Calculations

During the description phase of developing the program, the task to be performed should be processed manually and a list made of every calculation and/or manipulation. This list becomes an outline of the routines that must be included in the manipulation section of the program.

Describe the Calculation

Each calculation must be described in terms a person can understand.

As an example of this type of description, the instructions below show how the Payroll Program figures the earnings from the regular hours for week one.

Translate Into Program Lines

After the calculations have been carefully described, they can be translated into program lines. Three basic types of instructions are used to perform calculations and manipulations with the data: math functions, program controls, and String manipulations. These instructions and their respective translations are indicated below.

Math Functions

+ - Add the numeric values on the left to the numeric values on the right.

- - Subtract the numeric values on the right from the numeric values on the left.

* - Multiply the numeric values on the left by the numeric values on the right.

/ - Divide the numeric values on the left by the numeric values on the right.

INT(Numeric Value) - Convert the Numeric Value to a whole number by dropping off all values to the right of the decimal point.

Program Controls

FOR NEXT - Repeat the series of instructions between the FOR and the NEXT Instruction the designated number of times.

IF THEN - Compare the values between the IF and the THEN Instruction. Determine if the value to the left is equal to (=), greater than (>), or less than (<), the value to the right. If the results are found to be true, process the instructions to the right of the THEN Instruction.

GOTO - At this point, go to the designated location in the program.

GOSUB - At this point, go to the designated location in the program and perform the routine found there. Upon completion of the routine, return to this point and proceed to the next instruction.

ON GOTO - Go to one of the designated locations based on the value found between the ON and GOTO Instructions.

ON GOSUB - Go to one of the designated locations based on the value found between the ON and GOSUB Instructions and perform the routine found at this location. Upon completion, return to this point and proceed to the next instruction.

String Manipulation

VAL[String Value] - Convert the String Value to a numeric value.

STR$[Numeric Value] - Convert the Numeric Value to a String value.

LEN[String Value] - Report the number of characters in the String Value.

LEFT$[String Value, Numeric Value] - Count from the left to the right side of the String Value and drop off any characters from the right side that exceed the Numeric Value.

RIGHT$[String Value, Numeric Value] - Count from the right to the left side of the String Value and drop off any characters from the left side that exceed the Numeric Value.

MID$[String Value, 1st Value, 2nd Value] - Count from the left to the right side of the String Value until the number of characters represented by the 1st Value is reached. Drop off all the characters from the left side of the String Value up to this point. Now count over from the current position to the right side of the String Value by the amount in the 2nd Value. Drop off all characters from the right side of the String value, starting from the position reached using the 2nd Value.

Accessing the Manipulations

The program manipulations and calculations can be performed either after each transaction has been entered or after all of the information has been typed in. Some programs might perform a few calculations after each transaction has been entered, with additional calculations after all the data has been entered.

Calculations During Data Entry

To have the calculations performed at the end of each transaction, place a GOSUB Instruction just before the NEXT Instruction that directs the program to the next transaction. A RETURN Instruction must be included at the end of the calculation routine.

```
To Perform Calculations During Data Entry:

  1390 GOSUB 4000:REM  Program Calculations
  4000 REM  Begin Program Calculations
  4490 RETURN
```

Line 1390 is located as the last instruction before the NEXT Instruction in Line 1400. Lines 4000 and 4490 represent the calculation subroutine.

Calculations After Data Entry

When the calculations are performed after information is entered, place the GOSUB Instruction for the calculations after the NEXT Instruction. A FOR NEXT Loop must be used to process all of the transactions.

```
To Perform Calculations After Data Entry:

  1450 FOR X=1 TO LX
  1460 GOSUB 4000:REM  Program Calculations
  1470 NEXT X
  1480 RETURN
```

Program Output

After all of the information has been entered and manipulated, the program can produce the output. This output may be directed to the Video Screen, the printer, or the magnetic storage device. Each of these types of output requires a certain structure to the lines. This chapter describes those structures.

In addition to the actual output routines, a menu must be used to allow the Operator to specify the sequence of actions to be performed.

Menu of Functions

The menu lists each of the functions the program can perform by number. The Operator selects a number to activate an individual option. An ON GOSUB Instruction directs the program to the routine that performs that function. After the function is completed, the program returns to the menu which is redisplayed. The Operator can then select another option from those listed.

Menu of Functions:

```
800 CLS: REM  Alternate:  800 PRINT CHR$(12);
810 PRINT TAB(D1 + 11); "PROGRAM FUNCTIONS"
820 PRINT TAB(D1 + 11); "————————————————"
830 PRINT TAB(D1 + 6); "1) DISPLAY PROGRAM RECORDS"
840 PRINT TAB(D1 + 6); "2) DISPLAY PROGRAM RESULTS"
850 PRINT TAB(D1 + 6); "3) CORRECT ENTERED DATA"
870 PRINT TAB(D1 + 6); "5) PRINT TRANSACTIONS"
880 PRINT TAB(D1 + 6); "6) PRINT SUMMARY"
900 PRINT TAB(D1 + 6); "8) STORE DATA"
910 PRINT TAB(D1 + 6); "9) RETRIEVE DATA"
930 PRINT TAB(D1 + 5); "11) END THE PROGRAM"
940 PRINT: PRINT TAB(D1 + 11); "SELECT FUNCTION";
950 A$ = "": INPUT A$: A = VAL(A$)
960 IF A = 11 THEN GOTO 990
970 ON A GOSUB 2500,2000,3000,4000,5000,6000,7000,8000,9000
980 GOTO 800
990 PRINT: PRINT "THE END": END
```

Display Routines

Display routines use PRINT and TAB Instructions to present the information stored in Variables and Arrays in a meaningful format. The basic structure of this routine can be adapted for a variety of applications.

In the example below, a chart to the left of the program lines indicates the function of the various lines in the display. The terms used in this chart are described below.

Head – These lines display the headings that identify the items being displayed.

Data – This is the data that is displayed. It varies from one run of the program to the next.

Pause – When the information fills the display, this control stops the program so the Operator can see the current contents. The Enter Key is then pressed to continue the display. This control also occurs at the end of the display before the next function is processed.

Total – The information in the numeric Arrays can be totaled as it is being displayed. An initial line must first clear the Variables to be used for the totaling. Lines inside the FOR NEXT Loop accumulate the data. After all of the information has been processed, another line displays the totals.

HEAD	DATA	PAUSE	TOTAL	To Display Information:
			●	`2000 D = 0`
			●	`2005 V1 = 0:V2 = 0`
	●			`2010 FOR X = 1 TO LX`
●				`2020 IF D>0 THEN GOTO 2070`
●				`2030 CLS: REM  Alternate:  2030 PRINT CHR$(12);`
●				`2040 D = 3:PRINT TAB(D1 + 10);"INFORMATION DISPLAY":PRINT`
●				`2050 PRINT " #";TAB(5);"NAME";`
●				`2060 PRINT TAB(20);"VALUE 1";TAB(30);"VALUE 2"`
	●			`2070 REM Display Data`
	●			`2090 PRINT X;TAB(5);N1$(X);" ";N2$(X);`
	●			`2100 PRINT TAB(20);V1(X);TAB(30);V2(X)`
			●	`2105 V1 = V1 + V1(X):V2 = V2 + V2(X)`
		●		`2110 D = D + 1:IF D<D3 OR X = LX THEN GOTO 2130`
		●		`2120 GOSUB 2140:D = 0`
	●			`2130 NEXT X`
			●	`2132 PRINT TAB(20);"____________________"`
			●	`2134 PRINT TAB(20);V1;TAB(30);V2`
		●		`2140 PRINT:PRINT TAB(D1 + 6);"TO CONTINUE PRESS (ENTER)";`
		●		`2150 INPUT A$:RETURN`

Correct Data

A routine that allows the Operator to change information already entered should be added to this section.

The easiest way to accomplish this is to add a routine that uses the existing display routine. From this display, the Operator can select the transaction record to be changed. The program is then directed to the correction routine used during the entry process. The program lines below establish this type of routine.

To Correct Data:

```
2130 NEXT X:IF CX=1 THEN RETURN
3000 CX=1:GOSUB 2000
3010 PRINT:PRINT TAB(D1+7);"TO DISCONTINUE PRESS (ENTER)"
3020 PRINT TAB(D1+3);"SELECT NUMBER OF DATA TO CORRECT";
3030 A$="":INPUT A$:IF A$="" THEN GOTO 3050
3040 X=VAL(A$):GOSUB 3500:GOTO 3000
3050 CX=0:RETURN
```

Line 2130 modifies the display routine. The Variable CX at the end of the FOR NEXT Loop directs the program back to the correction routine rather than proceeding to the pause control in the display routine.

Line 3000 sets the value of the Variable CX to one when the correction routine begins. The program is then directed to the display routine.

At the end of the correction routine, Line 3050 restores the value of the Variable CX to zero.

Storage and Retrieval Routines

Storage and Retrieval routines must use the same sequence of lines for processing the data because the program must retrieve the information in the exact sequence in which it is stored. A variation of the PRINT Instruction records the data and the INPUT Instruction retrieves it.

In the example indicated below, charts to the left of the program lines indicate the functions of the various lines in these routines. The terms used in these charts are explained below.

Pause – The program informs the Operator that the storage device must be prepared for storage or retrieval.

Name – The name of the file to be processed is established.

Store – The data is stored.

Retrieve – The data is retrieved.

PAUSE	NAME	STORE	RETRIEVE	To Store Data:
•				8000 CLS: REM Alternate: 8000 PRINT CHR$(12);
•				8010 PRINT TAB(D1 + 9); "PREPARE TO STORE DATA"
•				8020 PRINT TAB(D1 + 4); "IS THE DISK READY (<Y> OR N)";
				(or)
•				8020 PRINT TAB(D1 + 2); "IS THE RECORDER READY (<Y> OR N)";
•				8030 A$ = "": INPUT A$: IF A$ = "N" OR A$ = "n" THEN RETURN
	•			8040 A$ = "XX" + TD$
			•	8050 OPEN "O",1,A$
			•	8060 PRINT#1,TD$
			•	8070 PRINT#1,LX
			•	8080 FOR X = 1 TO LX
			•	8090 PRINT#1,N1$(X)
			•	8100 PRINT#1,N2$(X)
			•	8110 PRINT#1,V1(X)
			•	8120 PRINT#1,V2(X)
			•	8130 NEXT X
			•	8140 CLOSE#1
				8150 RETURN

PAUSE	NAME	STORE	RETRIEVE	To Retrieve Data:
•				`9000 CLS: REM  Alternate:  9000 PRINT CHR$(12);`
•				`9010 PRINT TAB(D1+8);"PREPARE TO RETRIEVE DATA"`
•				`9020 PRINT TAB(D1+4);"IS THE DISK READY (<Y> OR N)";`
				(or)
•				`9020 PRINT TAB(D1+2);"IS THE RECORDER READY (<Y> OR N)";`
•				`9030 A$="":INPUT A$:IF A$="N" OR A$="n" THEN RETURN`
	•			`9040 A$="XX"+TD$`
			•	`9050 OPEN "I",1,A$`
			•	`9060 INPUT#1,TD$`
			•	`9070 INPUT#1,LX`
			•	`9080 FOR X=1 TO LX`
			•	`9090 INPUT#1,N1$(X)`
			•	`9100 INPUT#1,N2$(X)`
			•	`9110 INPUT#1,V1(X)`
			•	`9120 INPUT#1,V2(X)`
			•	`9130 NEXT X`
			•	`9140 CLOSE#1`
				`9150 RETURN`

Lines 8040 and 9040 establish the file name for the data by combining a short program identifier, "XX", with the date. Other variations for establishing the file name, such as an INPUT Instruction, can be used.

PRINT ROUTINES

The basic subroutines for printing information can be used exactly as described for the Payroll Program. These subroutines open and close the communication channels to the printer, direct individual lines of copy to the printer, and prepare the horizontal and vertical positions of the information on the page.

After establishing the basic print routines, two types of forms can be generated: Records of Individual Transactions and Summaries of Transactions.

Basic Printing Subroutines

The basic printing subroutines can be used without modification. In the example below, a chart to the left of the program lines indicates the functions of the various lines. The terms used in this chart are described below.

Open – This routine opens the communication channel to the printer before the printing commences.

Print – This subroutine directs individual lines of copy to the printer.

Close – The communication channel to the printer is closed.

Stop – This subroutine allows the Operator to stop the print routine by pressing the Space Bar.

VT – The Vertical Tab subroutine advances the paper out of the printer to a vertical position on the page.

Right Tab – Information is added to the current line with the placement adjusted to the right side of the data.

$ Format – The data is converted to a dollar format.

Left Tab – Information is added to the current line with the placement adjusted to the left side of the data.

OPEN	PRINT	CLOSE	STOP	Basic Printing Subroutines:
			•	120 IN = 0 : A$ = INKEY$: IF A$ = " " THEN IN = 1
			•	125 RETURN
•				130 OPEN "LPT1 :" AS #2 : WIDTH#2,255
•				135 RETURN
	•			140 PRINT#2,P$: REM Alternate: 140 PRINT#2,P$; CHR$(10)
	•			145 PL = PL + 1 : RETURN
		•		150 CLOSE#2
		•		155 RETURN

VT	RIGHT TAB	$ FORMAT	LEFT TAB	**Tab Routines:**
•				`160 PD = VT – PL : IF PD <1 THEN RETURN`
•				`170 P$ = " " : FOR A = 1 TO PD : GOSUB 140 : NEXT A : RETURN`
	•		•	`300 FOR X = 1 TO 120 : SP$ = SP$ + CHR$(32) : LN$ = LN$ + "–" : NEXT X`
	•	•		`5900 A$ = SP$ : GOTO 5920 : REM  Tab Right with Dollar Format`
	•	•		`5910 A$ = SP$ + "$" : REM  Tab Right with "$"`
		•		`5920 A = INT(100 * V + .5)/100 : VA$ = STR$(A) : VI$ = STR$(INT(A))`
		•		`5930 IF LEN(VA$) = LEN(VI$) THEN VA$ = VA$ + "."`
		•		`5940 L = LEN(VI$) + 3 : IF A > 0 AND A < 1 THEN L = L – 1`
		•		`5950 VA$ = VA$ + "00" : A$ = A$ + MID$(VA$,2,L – 1)`
		•		`5951 REM  Alternate: 5950 VA$ = VA$ + "00" : A$ = A$ + MID$(VA$,1,L)`
	•			`5960 P$ = LEFT$(P$,TB) : TB = TB – LEN(P$)`
	•			`5970 P$ = P$ + RIGHT$(A$,TB) : RETURN`
	•			`5980 A$ = SP$ + A$ : GOTO 5960 : REM  Tab Right.  No Dollar Format`
			•	`5990 P$ = P$ + SP$ : P$ = LEFT$(P$,TB) + A$ : RETURN : REM  Tab Left`

FORMAT FOR LINES USING TAB ROUTINES

Vertical Tab
`0000 VT = 00 : GOSUB 160`

Tab Right with Dollar Format
`0000 V = 0.00 : TB = 00 : GOSUB 5900`

Tab Right with Dollar Format and Dollar Sign ($)
`0000 V = 0.00 : TB = 00 : GOSUB 5910`

Tab Right with no Dollar Format
`0000 A$ = "…" : TB = 00 : GOSUB 5980`

Tab Left with no Dollar Format
`0000 A$ = "…" : TB = 00 : GOSUB 5990`

Variables:
- A$ – Copy to be added to line
- TB – Horizontal distance from left margin of page
- VT – Vertical distance from top of page
- V – Numeric value to be converted to Dollar Format
- P$ – Line to be printed

(To start a new line this Variable should be cleared, P$ = "")
`0000 P$ = "" : V = 0.00 : TB = 00 : GOSUB 5910`

Printing Records

The routines required to print records of individual transactions and summaries of transactions can be created using the structure shown on these two pages.

In these examples, a chart to the left of the program lines indicates the functions of the various lines. The terms used in this chart are described below.

Pause – The program informs the Operator of the printing function to be performed. The program is then halted until the Operator specifies that the paper is in place and the printer is turned on.

Process – The program proceeds from one transaction to the next until all of the transactions are processed.

Head – These lines print the headings that identify the information being printed.

Data – The information created by the program is printed.

Total – Information from each column containing numeric data is totaled and the results are printed at the bottom of the page.

PAUSE	PROCESS	DATA	To Print Individual Records of Transactions:
•			`5000 CLS: REM  Alternate:  5000 PRINT CHR$(12);`
•			`5010 PRINT TAB(D1 + 5);"PREPARE TO PRINT TRANSACTIONS"`
•			`5020 PRINT TAB(D1 + 3);"IS THE PRINTER READY ( <Y> OR N)";`
•			`5030 A$ = "":INPUT A$:IF A$ = "N" OR A$ = "n" THEN RETURN`
	•		`5040 PRINT TAB(D1 + 5);"TO STOP PRINTER PRESS (SPACE)"`
	•		`5050 GOSUB 130:REM  Initialize Printer`
	•		`5060 FOR X = 1 TO LX`
	•		`5090 GOSUB 5500:IF IN = 1 THEN GOTO 5110`
	•		`5100 NEXT X`
	•		`5110 GOSUB 150:RETURN`
		•	`5500 VS = 2:PL = VS:REM  Starting Line`
		•	`5510 VT = 6:GOSUB 160:REM  First Vertical Line`
		•	`5515 GOSUB 120:IF IN = 1 THEN RETURN`
		•	`5520 P$ = "":A$ = "COMPANY NAME":TB = 5:GOSUB 5990`
		•	`5530 GOSUB 140:GOSUB 120:IF IN = 1 THEN RETURN`
		•	`5540 P$ = "":A$ = "123 Main Street":TB = 5:GOSUB 5990`
		•	`5550 GOSUB 140:GOSUB 120:IF IN = 1 THEN RETURN`
		•	`5560 P$ = "":A$ = "This Town, State 98950":TB = 5:GOSUB 5990`
		•	`5570 GOSUB 140:VT = 12:GOSUB 160`
		•	`5575 GOSUB 120:IF IN = 1 THEN RETURN`
		•	`5600 P$ = "":A$ = "RECEIVED FROM:":TB = 5:GOSUB 5990`
		•	`5610 GOSUB 140:VT = 14:GOSUB 160`
		•	`5615 GOSUB 120:IF IN = 1 THEN RETURN`
		•	`5620 P$ = "":A$ = N1$(X) + " " + N2$(X):TB = 5:GOSUB 5990`
		•	`5630 V = V1(X):TB = 25:GOSUB 5900:REM  Value 1`
		•	`5640 V = V2(X):TB = 35:GOSUB 5900:REM  Value 2`
		•	`5650 GOSUB 140:VT = 20 + VS:GOSUB 160`
		•	`5660 RETURN`

To Print a Summary of the Transactions:

PAUSE	PROCESS	HEAD	DATA	TOTAL	
•					`6000 CLS: REM  Alternate:  6000 PRINT CHR$(12);`
•					`6010 PRINT TAB(D1 + 5);"PREPARE TO PRINT DATA SUMMARY"`
•					`6020 PRINT TAB(D1 + 3);"IS THE PRINTER READY (<Y> OR N)";`
•					`6030 A$ = "":INPUT A$:IF A$ = "N" OR A$ = "n" THEN RETURN`
	•				`6040 PRINT TAB(D1 + 5);"TO STOP PRINTER PRESS (SPACE)"`
	•				`6050 GOSUB 130:PL = 0:REM  Initialize Printing`
				•	`6055 V1 = 0:V2 = 0`
	•				`6060 FOR X = 1 TO LX`
		•			`6070 IF PL > 0 THEN GOTO 6090`
		•			`6080 GOSUB 6500:IF IN = 1 THEN GOTO 6170:REM  Print Heading`
			•		`6090 REM  Begin Data`
				•	`6105 V1 = V1 + V1(X):V2 = V2 + V2(X)`
			•		`6110 GOSUB 6700:IF IN = 1 THEN GOTO 6170:REM  Print Data`
•					`6120 IF PL < 51 − 6 THEN GOTO 6160`
•					`6130 PRINT TAB(D1 + 6);"PUT IN A NEW SHEET OF PAPER"`
•					`6140 PRINT TAB(D1 + 6);"TO CONTINUE PRESS (ENTER)";`
•					`6150 INPUT A$:PL = 0`
	•				`6160 NEXT X`
				•	`6165 GOSUB 6800:REM  Print Totals`
	•				`6170 GOSUB 150:RETURN`
		•			`6500 VS = 2:PL = VS:REM  Starting Line`
		•			`6510 VT = 6:GOSUB 160:REM  First Vertical Line`
		•			`6515 GOSUB 120:IF IN = 1 THEN RETURN`
		•			`6520 P$ = "":A$ = "DATA SUMMARY FOR " + TD$`
		•			`6530 TB = INT((85 − LEN(A$))/2):GOSUB 5990`
		•			`6540 GOSUB 140:GOSUB 120:IF IN = 1 THEN RETURN`
		•			`6580 P$ = " ":GOSUB 140`
		•			`6600 P$ = "":A$ = " #":TB = 5:GOSUB 5990`
		•			`6610 A$ = "Name":TB = 10:GOSUB 5990`
		•			`6620 A$ = "Value 1":TB = 35:GOSUB 5980`
		•			`6630 A$ = "Value 2":TB = 45:GOSUB 5980`
		•			`6695 GOSUB 140:P$ = " ":GOSUB 140:GOSUB 120:RETURN`
			•		`6700 P$ = "":A$ = STR$(X):TB = 5:GOSUB 5990:REM  #`
			•		`6710 A$ = N1$(X) + " " + N2$(X):TB = 10:GOSUB 5990:REM  Name`
			•		`6720 V = V1(X):TB = 35:GOSUB 5900:REM  Value 1`
			•		`6730 V = V2(X):TB = 45:GOSUB 5900:REM  Value 2`
			•		`6795 GOSUB 140:GOSUB 120:RETURN`
				•	`6800 P$ = "":A$ = LEFT$(LN$,20):TB = 45:GOSUB 5980:REM  Line`
				•	`6810 GOSUB 140:GOSUB 120:IF IN = 1 THEN RETURN`
				•	`6820 P$ = "":V = V1:TB = 35:GOSUB 5910:REM  Value 1`
				•	`6830 V = V2:TB = 45:GOSUB 5910:REM  Value 2`
				•	`6895 GOSUB 140:RETURN`

Appendix A

CALIFORNIA STATE DEDUCTION ALLOWANCE

```
STEP (1)    IF THE EMPLOYEE CLAIMS ANY ADDITIONAL WITHHOLDING ALLOWANCES FOR
            ESTIMATED DEDUCTIONS, SUBTRACT THE AMOUNT SHOWN IN "TABLE A -
            ESTIMATED DEDUCTION TABLE" FROM THE GROSS SALARIES AND WAGES.
```

Step 1 of the California Employer's Tax Guide allows employees to declare additional tax exemptions for estimated deductions. To include this in the Payroll Program, the READ and DATA Instructions must be expanded to include the additional data. The Variable Z is used in the READ Instruction to retrieve the new California exemption. The Employee Record display must also be extended to include the new exemption. The following lines make these modifications to the existing program.

California Deduction Allowance - Program Changes:

```
2560 PRINT TAB(27);MAR;TAB(32);EX;TAB(36);CODE;
2565 PRINT TAB(42);CA EX
2590 PRINT TAB(27);M;TAB(32);X;TAB(36);C;TAB(42);Z
9500 READ E,N$,F$,P,M,X,C,S$,Z
9555 REM Ca Ex: Special California Deduction Exemption
9600 REM #,Last Name,First Name,Pay,Mar,Ex,Code,Soc Sec,CA Ex
9610 DATA 1, Harrison, James, 5.25, 1, 1, 1, 606-03-7378, 0
9620 DATA 2, Samuels, Barbara, 5.50, 3, 4, 1, 498-27-6249, 5
9630 DATA 3, Johnson, Louis, 5.75, 2, 2, 1, 534-65-1032, 2
```

Line 2560 is already a part of the program. The only change is adding a semi-colon (;) to the end of the line.

Line 2565 adds the heading for the new exemption.

Line 2590 adds the Variable Z for the new data when the information about each employee is displayed.

Line 9500 modifies the existing READ Instruction so it will retrieve the new exemption.

Lines 9610 to 9630 must be modified to add the California exemption for each employee even if the value is only zero.

```
                  TABLE A - ESTIMATED DEDUCTION TABLE
```

ADDITIONAL WITHHOLDING ALLOWANCES+	WEEKLY	BI-WEEKLY	SEMI-MONTHLY	MONTHLY	QUARTERLY	SEMI-ANNUAL	ANNUAL	DAILY/MISC.
1	19	38	42	83	250	500	1000	4
2	38	77	83	167	500	1000	2000	8
3	58	115	125	250	750	1500	3000	12
4	77	154	167	333	1000	2000	4000	15
5	96	192	208	417	1250	2500	5000	19
6	115	231	250	500	1500	3000	6000	23
7	135	269	292	583	1750	3500	7000	27
8	154	308	333	667	2000	4000	8000	31
9	173	346	375	750	2250	4500	9000	35
10*	192	385	417	833	2500	5000	10000	38

```
+   NUMBER OF ADDITIONAL WITHHOLDING ALLOWANCES FOR ESTIMATED DEDUCTIONS
    CLAIMED ON FORM DE-4 OR W-4.

*   IF THE NUMBER OF ADDITIONAL WITHHOLDING ALLOWANCES FOR ESTIMATED DEDUCTIONS CLAIMED
    IS GREATER THAN 10, MULTIPLY THE AMOUNT SHOWN FOR ONE ADDITIONAL WITHHOLDING
    ALLOWANCE BY THE NUMBER CLAIMED.
```

The calculation for Step 1 is performed by subtracting a deduction allowance from the Gross Pay. The specific amount to be deducted is determined from Table A using the number of allowances claimed by the employee. The following steps perform this computation.

California Deduction Allowance - Table A:

```
4300 S = GP(E):IF Z = 0 THEN GOTO 4400
4305 ON Z GOTO 4311,4312,4313,4314,4315,4316,4317,4318,4319,4320
4310 GOTO 4321
4311 S = S - 38:GOTO 4400
4312 S = S - 77:GOTO 4400
4313 S = S - 115:GOTO 4400
4314 S = S - 134:GOTO 4400
4315 S = S - 192:GOTO 4400
4316 S = S - 231:GOTO 4400
4317 S = S - 269:GOTO 4400
4318 S = S - 308:GOTO 4400
4319 S = S - 346:GOTO 4400
4320 S = S - 385:GOTO 4400
4321 S = S - Z * 38
4420 S = S - 58:GOTO 4450
4440 S = S - 116
```

Lines 4300 to 4321 adjust the taxable income for California residents based on the deduction allowance.

Lines 4420 and 4440 are already a part of the Payroll Program. They originally determined the taxable income by subtracting a standard deduction from the Gross Pay Array, GP(E), see page 102. They are modified here to subtract the standard deduction from the taxable income determined by Lines 4300 to 4321.

Appendix B

COMPUTER FORMS

A variety of forms have been designed expressly for use with computers. These forms may simply be continuous-form 3-by-5-inch file cards or specially imprinted checks such as the one indicated on the opposite page. A list of firms that sell computer forms by mail is indicated below.

The paycheck on page 215 and the W-2 forms on page 216 are reproduced so the printing routines described in this book can be tested.

Deluxe Computer Forms
530 N. Wheeler St.
P.O. Box 43046
St. Paul, MN 55164

800-328-0304

Moore Computer Forms
P.O. Box 20
Wheeling, IL 60090

800-323-6230

NEBS Computer Forms
12 South Street
Townsend, MA 01469

800-225-9550

Rapidforms, Inc.
501 Benigno Blvd.
Bellmawr, NJ 08031

800-257-8354

Streamliners
P.O. Box 480
5215 E. Simpson Ferry Road
Mechanicsburg, PA 17055

800-233-1190

Uarco Computer Supplies
121 North Ninth Street
DeKalb, IL 60115

800-435-0713

Visible Computer Supply Corp.
3626 Stern Drive
St. Charles, IL 60174

800-323-0628

Product 9000, Available from NEBS Computer Forms
12 South Street, Townsend, MA 01469

1 Control number		OMB No. 1545-0008	

2 Employer's name, address, and ZIP code	**3** Employer's identification number	**4** Employer's State number

	5 Stat. employee ☐ Deceased ☐ Legal rep. ☐ 942 emp. ☐ Subtotal ☐ Void ☐

6 Allocated tips	**7** Advance EIC payment

8 Employee's social security number	**9** Federal income tax withheld	**10** Wages, tips, other compensation	**11** Social security tax withheld

12 Employee's name, address, and ZIP code	**13** Social security wages	**14** Social security tips

16

17 State income tax	**18** State wages, tips, etc.	**19** Name of State
20 Local income tax	**21** Local wages, tips, etc.	**22** Name of locality

Form **W-2 Wage and Tax Statement** **1984**   Copy 1 For State, City, or Local Tax Department
Employee's and employer's copy compared ☐

- -

1 Control number		OMB No. 1545-0008	

2 Employer's name, address, and ZIP code	**3** Employer's identification number	**4** Employer's State number

	5 Stat. employee ☐ Deceased ☐ Legal rep. ☐ 942 emp. ☐ Subtotal ☐ Void ☐

6 Allocated tips	**7** Advance EIC payment

8 Employee's social security number	**9** Federal income tax withheld	**10** Wages, tips, other compensation	**11** Social security tax withheld

12 Employee's name, address, and ZIP code	**13** Social security wages	**14** Social security tips

16

17 State income tax	**18** State wages, tips, etc.	**19** Name of State
20 Local income tax	**21** Local wages, tips, etc.	**22** Name of locality

Form **W-2 Wage and Tax Statement** **1984**   Copy 1 For State, City, or Local Tax Department
Employee's and employer's copy compared ☐

- -

1 Control number		OMB No. 1545-0008	

2 Employer's name, address, and ZIP code	**3** Employer's identification number	**4** Employer's State number

	5 Stat. employee ☐ Deceased ☐ Legal rep. ☐ 942 emp. ☐ Subtotal ☐ Void ☐

6 Allocated tips	**7** Advance EIC payment

8 Employee's social security number	**9** Federal income tax withheld	**10** Wages, tips, other compensation	**11** Social security tax withheld

12 Employee's name, address, and ZIP code	**13** Social security wages	**14** Social security tips

16

17 State income tax	**18** State wages, tips, etc.	**19** Name of State
20 Local income tax	**21** Local wages, tips, etc.	**22** Name of locality

Appendix C

FEDERAL TAX TABLES

The complete federal Tax Tables for 1984 are reproduced on the following two pages for readers who wish to try the program variations suggested on pages 154 to 159.

Tables for Percentage Method of Withholding

(For Wages Paid After June 1983 and Before January 1985)

TABLE 1—If the Payroll Period with Respect to an Employee is Weekly

(a) SINGLE person—including head of household:

If the amount of wages is:

Not over $27 0

The amount of income tax to be withheld shall be:

Over—	But not over—		of excess over—
$27	—$79	12%	—$27
$79	—$183	$6.24 plus 15%	—$79
$183	—$277	$21.84 plus 19%	—$183
$277	—$423	$39.70 plus 25%	—$277
$423	—$535	$76.20 plus 30%	—$423
$535	—$637	$109.80 plus 34%	—$535
$637		$144.48 plus 37%	—$637

(b) MARRIED person—

If the amount of wages is:

Not over $46 0

The amount of income tax to be withheld shall be:

Over—	But not over—		of excess over—
$46	—$185	12%	—$46
$185	—$369	$16.68 plus 17%	—$185
$369	—$454	$47.96 plus 22%	—$369
$454	—$556	$66.66 plus 25%	—$454
$556	—$658	$92.16 plus 28%	—$556
$658	—$862	$120.72 plus 33%	—$658
$862		$188.04 plus 37%	—$862

TABLE 2—If the Payroll Period With Respect to an Employee is Biweekly

(a) SINGLE person—including head of household:

If the amount of wages is:

Not over $54 0

The amount of income tax to be withheld shall be:

Over—	But not over—		of excess over—
$54	—$158	12%	—$54
$158	—$365	$12.48 plus 15%	—$158
$365	—$554	$43.53 plus 19%	—$365
$554	—$846	$79.44 plus 25%	—$554
$846	—$1,069	$152.44 plus 30%	—$846
$1,069	—$1,273	$219.34 plus 34%	—$1,069
$1,273		$288.70 plus 37%	—$1,273

(b) MARRIED person—

If the amount of wages is:

Not over $92 0

The amount of income tax to be withheld shall be:

Over—	But not over—		of excess over—
$92	—$369	12%	—$92
$369	—$738	$33.24 plus 17%	—$369
$738	—$908	$95.97 plus 22%	—$738
$908	—$1,112	$133.37 plus 25%	—$908
$1,112	—$1,315	$184.37 plus 28%	—$1,112
$1,315	—$1,723	$241.21 plus 33%	—$1,315
$1,723		$375.85 plus 37%	—$1,723

TABLE 3—If the Payroll Period With Respect to an Employee is Semimonthly

(a) SINGLE person—including head of household:

If the amount of wages is:

Not over $58 0

The amount of income tax to be withheld shall be:

Over—	But not over—		of excess over—
$58	—$171	12%	—$58
$171	—$396	$13.56 plus 15%	—$171
$396	—$600	$47.31 plus 19%	—$396
$600	—$917	$86.07 plus 25%	—$600
$917	—$1,158	$165.32 plus 30%	—$917
$1,158	—$1,379	$237.62 plus 34%	—$1,158
$1,379		$312.76 plus 37%	—$1,379

(b) MARRIED person—

If the amount of wages is:

Not over $100 0

The amount of income tax to be withheld shall be:

Over—	But not over—		of excess over—
$100	—$400	12%	—$100
$400	—$799	$36.00 plus 17%	—$400
$799	—$983	$103.83 plus 22%	—$799
$983	—$1,204	$144.31 plus 25%	—$983
$1,204	—$1,425	$199.56 plus 28%	—$1,204
$1,425	—$1,867	$261.44 plus 33%	—$1,425
$1,867		$407.30 plus 37%	—$1,867

TABLE 4—If the Payroll Period With Respect to an Employee is Monthly

(a) SINGLE person—including head of household:

If the amount of wages is:

Not over $117 0

The amount of income tax to be withheld shall be:

Over—	But not over—		of excess over—
$117	—$342	12%	—$117
$342	—$792	$27.00 plus 15%	—$342
$792	—$1,200	$94.50 plus 19%	—$792
$1,200	—$1,833	$172.02 plus 25%	—$1,200
$1,833	—$2,317	$330.27 plus 30%	—$1,833
$2,317	—$2,758	$475.47 plus 34%	—$2,317
$2,758		$625.41 plus 37%	—$2,758

(b) MARRIED person—

If the amount of wages is:

Not over $200 0

The amount of income tax to be withheld shall be:

Over—	But not over—		of excess over—
$200	—$800	12%	—$200
$800	—$1,598	$72.00 plus 17%	—$800
$1,598	—$1,967	$207.66 plus 22%	—$1,598
$1,967	—$2,408	$288.84 plus 25%	—$1,967
$2,408	—$2,850	$399.09 plus 28%	—$2,408
$2,850	—$3,733	$522.85 plus 33%	—$2,850
$3,733		$814.24 plus 37%	—$3,733

(For Wages Paid After June 1983 and Before January 1985)

TABLE 5—If the Payroll Period With Respect to an Employee is Quarterly

(a) SINGLE person—including head of household:

If the amount of wages is: / The amount of income tax to be withheld shall be:

Not over $350 0

Over—	But not over—		of excess over—
$350	—$1,025	...12%	—$350
$1,025	—$2,375	...$81.00 plus 15%	—$1,025
$2,375	—$3,600	...$283.50 plus 19%	—$2,375
$3,600	—$5,500	...$516.25 plus 25%	—$3,600
$5,500	—$6,950	...$991.25 plus 30%	—$5,500
$6,950	—$8,275	...$1,426.25 plus 34%	—$6,950
$8,275		...........$1,876.75 plus 37%	—$8,275

(b) MARRIED person—

If the amount of wages is: / The amount of income tax to be withheld shall be:

Not over $600 0

Over—	But not over—		of excess over—
$600	—$2,400	...12%	—$600
$2,400	—$4,795	...$216.00 plus 17%	—$2,400
$4,795	—$5,900	...$623.15 plus 22%	—$4,795
$5,900	—$7,225	..$866.25 plus 25%	—$5,900
$7,225	—$8,550	...$1,197.50 plus 28%	—$7,225
$8,550	—$11,200	..$1,568.50 plus 33%	—$8,550
$11,200		...........$2,443.00 plus 37%	—$11,200

TABLE 6—If the Payroll Period With Respect to an Employee is Semiannual

(a) SINGLE person—including head of household:

If the amount of wages is: / The amount of income tax to be withheld shall be:

Not over $700 0

Over—	But not over—		of excess over—
$700	—$2,050	...12%	—$700
$2,050	—$4,750	..$162.00 plus 15%	—$2,050
$4,750	—$7,200	..$567.00 plus 19%	—$4,750
$7,200	—$11,000	..$1,032.50 plus 25%	—$7,200
$11,000	—$13,900	..$1,982.50 plus 30%	—$11,000
$13,900	—$16,550	..$2,852.50 plus 34%	—$13,900
$16,550		..........$3,753.50 plus 37%	—$16,550

(b) MARRIED person—

If the amount of wages is: / The amount of income tax to be withheld shall be:

Not over $1,200 0

Over—	But not over—		of excess over—
$1,200	—$4,800	...12%	—$1,200
$4,800	—$9,590	...$432.00 plus 17%	—$4,800
$9,590	—$11,800	..$1,246.30 plus 22%	—$9,590
$11,800	—$14,450	..$1,732.50 plus 25%	—$11,800
$14,450	—$17,100	..$2,395.00 plus 28%	—$14,450
$17,100	—$22,400	..$3,137.00 plus 33%	—$17,100
$22,400		...........$4,886.00 plus 37%	—$22,400

TABLE 7—If the Payroll Period With Respect to an Employee is Annual

(a) SINGLE person—including head of household:

If the amount of wages is: / The amount of income tax to be withheld shall be:

Not over $1,400 0

Over—	But not over—		of excess over—
$1,400	—$4,100	...12%	—$1,400
$4,100	—$9,500	..$324.00 plus 15%	—$4,100
$9,500	—$14,400	..$1,134.00 plus 19%	—$9,500
$14,400	—$22,000	..$2,065.00 plus 25%	—$14,400
$22,000	—$27,800	..$3,965.00 plus 30%	—$22,000
$27,800	—$33,100	..$5,705.00 plus 34%	—$27,800
$33,100		..........$7,507.00 plus 37%	—$33,100

(b) MARRIED person—

If the amount of wages is: / The amount of income tax to be withheld shall be:

Not over $2,400 0

Over—	But not over—		of excess over—
$2,400	—$9,600	...12%	—$2,400
$9,600	—$19,180	..$864.00 plus 17%	—$9,600
$19,180	—$23,600	..$2,492.60 plus 22%	—$19,180
$23,600	—$28,900	..$3,465.00 plus 25%	—$23,600
$28,900	—$34,200	..$4,790.00 plus 28%	—$28,900
$34,200	—$44,800	..$6,274.00 plus 33%	—$34,200
$44,800		...........$9,772.00 plus 37%	—$44,800

TABLE 8—If the Payroll Period With Respect to an Employee is a Daily Payroll Period or a Miscellaneous Payroll Period

(a) SINGLE person—including head of household:

If the amount of wages divided by the number of days in the payroll period is: / The amount of income tax to be withheld shall be:

Not over $5.40 0

Over—	But not over—		of excess over—
$5.40	—$15.80	...12%	—$5.40
$15.80	—$36.50	...$1.25 plus 15%	—$15.80
$36.50	—$55.40	...$4.36 plus 19%	—$36.50
$55.40	—$84.60	...$7.95 plus 25%	—$55.40
$84.60	—$106.90	.$15.25 plus 30%	—$84.60
$106.90	—$127.30	.$21.94 plus 34%	—$106.90
$127.30		..........$28.88 plus 37%	—$127.30

(b) MARRIED person—

If the amount of wages divided by the number of days in the payroll period is: / The amount of income tax to be withheld shall be:

Not over $9.20 0

Over—	But not over—		of excess over—
$9.20	—$36.90	...12%	—$9.20
$36.90	—$73.80	...$3.32 plus 17%	—$36.90
$73.80	—$90.80	...$9.59 plus 22%	—$73.80
$90.80	—$111.20	.$13.33 plus 25%	—$90.80
$111.20	—$131.50	..$18.43 plus 28%	—$111.20
$131.50	—$172.30	..$24.11 plus 33%	—$131.50
$172.30		.........$37.57 plus 37%	—$172.30

Glossary

Arrays	Locations in the computer's memory that hold a vast "array" of information. A specific Variable within the Array is selected by the numeric value that appears between the parentheses of the Array name, A( ).
CLS	The Video Screen is cleared and the Cursor moves to the top left corner of the display.
Colon (:)	Separates two instructions in a program line.
COPY	Copies the contents of one Disk on to a second Disk.
CLOSE	Closes the communication channel to Cassette Tape Recorders, Disk Drives, and printers.
Cursor	A graphic character that appears on the screen to indicate where the next character will appear.
DATA	An instruction used to store information in a program that will later be retrieved by a READ Instruction.
DATE$	Returns the current date.
DELETE	Deletes a sequence of lines from a program.
DIM	Dimensions the number of Variables to be used in an Array.
DIR	Displays the names of the programs and data stored on a Disk.
END	Terminates the operation of a program and returns control of the computer to BASIC.
File Name	A label assigned to individual programs and information stored on Disk.
FOR	The beginning instruction of a FOR NEXT Loop that informs the computer to perform the instructions in the loop a specified number of times.
FORMAT	Formats a Disk so information and programs can be stored on it.
GOSUB	Directs the program to a subroutine beginning at a specified Line Number. When the subroutine is completed, the program proceeds to the instruction immediately following the GOSUB Instruction.
GOTO	Directs the computer to a specified Line Number in a program.
Greater Than	Included between the IF and the THEN Instructions to determine if the value to the left of the sign is greater than the value to the right.
IF THEN	Performs a comparison of the values between the IF and the THEN Instructions and controls the actions to the right of the THEN Instruction based on these results.
INKEY$	Retrieves the character of a single key as soon as it is pressed.
INPUT	Accepts information from the Keyboard until the Return/Enter Key is pressed.
INPUT#	Retrieves information from Cassette Tape Recorder or Disk Drive.
INT	Returns the integer of a numeric value by eliminating values to the right of the decimal point.
LEFT$	Returns the characters from the left side of a String to a length specified by a numeric value.
LEN	Determines the number of characters in a String.
Less Than	Included between the IF and the THEN Instruction to determine if the value to the left of the sign is less than the value to the right of the sign.
Line Numbers	Numbers assigned to the beginning of BASIC Instructions so the instructions will be stored in the computer's memory as a program.
LIST	Displays the lines of a program on the Video Screen.
LLIST	Prints the lines of a program.
LOAD	Loads a program from Cassette Tape or Disk into the computer's memory.
MID$	Returns the middle portion of a String starting from a location specified by a numeric value. The length of the String returned is controlled by a second numeric value.

NEW	Clears a program from the computer's memory.
NEXT	The last instruction in a FOR NEXT Loop that returns the program to the first instruction in the loop until a specified numeric value is achieved.
ON GOSUB	A numeric value between the ON and the GOSUB Instruction is used to count over to a specified Line Number to the right of the GOSUB Instruction. The program proceeds to the the subroutine beginning at this Line Number. When the subroutine is terminated by aRETURN Instruction, the program returns to the instruction immediately following the ON GOSUB Instruction.
ON GOTO	A numeric value between the ON and the GOTO Instruction that is used to count over to a specified Line Number to the right of the GOTO Instruction. The program proceeds to the specified Line Number.
OPEN	Opens a communication channel to a Cassette Tape Recorder, Disk Drive, or printer.
OR	Included between the IF and the THEN Instructions, the OR Instruction allows more than one value comparison to be made.
Parentheses	The sequence of math functions to be performed is controlled by placing the computations to be performed first between parentheses.
PRINT	Information is displayed on the Video Screen.
PRINT#	Information is directed to a Cassette Tape Recorder, Disk Drive, or printer.
PRINT USING	A numeric value is displayed in a format that is controlled by a String expression on the right side of the USING Instruction.
READ	Information is retrieved from DATA Instructions.
REM	Information about a program's design is stored following the REM Instruction. These comments do not affect the operation of the program.
RESTORE	The program is directed to start retrieving information from the first DATA Instruction when the next READ Instruction is encountered.
RETURN	This instruction terminates subroutines accessed by GOSUB Instructions. It returns control of the program to the originating GOSUB Instruction.
RIGHT$	Returns the characters from the right side of a String to a length specified by a numeric value.
RUN	Initiates the operation of the program in the computer's memory.
SAVE	Stores the program in the computer's memory on a Cassette Tape or Disk.
Semi-colon (;)	Separates numeric values and Strings in PRINT Instructions.
STR$	Converts a numeric value to a String.
String	Information that is stored in the computer's memory as a literal sequence of characters.
Subroutines	A routine that performs a specific function within a program. These routines are usually accessed from several different locations in the program by GOSUB Instructions.
TAB	Controls the horizontal placement of information on the display.
VAL	Returns the numeric value of a String.
Variables	Storage locations in the computer's memory that may contain either numeric values or Strings of characters.

Index

WRITE, EDIT, & PRINT
Word Processing with Personal Computers
with
THE WORD WORKER ® Programs
by Donald H. McCunn

Write, Edit, & Print
Selected as one of the Best Sci-Tech Books published in 1982 by
    Library Journal
A Selection of the American Management Association Book Club

The Word Worker ®
"I'd give it a 10 for value" — PC Magazine
"... more than worth the price." — In Business

Write, Edit, & Print extends the concepts described in this book to word processing—the single most popular personal computer application. It offers a practical buyer's guide to computers and printers, plus four fully annotated word processing programs from **The Word Worker ®** system. These programs are presented as short type-in-and-enter routines that allow testing of individual functions as the overall programs are created. Variations are included to illustrate how small changes to the program can dramatically alter the performance of the equipment. These programs may be used "as is" for standard word processing applications or modified to individual requirements.

For people who do not want to type in the programs, a book/disk combination provides **The Word Worker ®** programs on disk for the most popular computer systems including the Apple II/IIe/IIc, The Commodore 64/PET/CBM, IBM PC/PCjr, TRS-80 I/III. The MS-DOS book/disk can be used with a wide variety of computers that are IBM data compatible including Columbia, Compaq, IBM, Tandy 2000, Televideo Tele-PC, Texas Instruments Professional, Wang PC, Zenith Z-100, and the Zenith Z-150.

"This is word processing for the masses. In addition, the system can easily be modified; in effect, you can ... essentially customize the system's operation to your best advantage."
> — EPB: Electronic Publishing & Bookselling

"... it gives one of the clearest and most intelligible explanations of a complex BASIC program I've seen."
> — PC Magazine

"Some **Word Worker ®** features are absent even from the most expensive word processors."
> — Infoworld

"It is a beautiful program. It's simplicity and thorough coverage of all aspects of word processing are exciting."
> — Elwin R. Hewitt, Pastor

"We have been using the product for 18 months and it has satisfied our word processing requirements for business, school, and personal communications. I quickly and easily implemented my word processor, have used it every business day for 18 months without one program fault and am completely satisfied with a quality product."
> Pat Patterson, President, World Trade Associates

Forthcoming Titles

WRITE, EDIT, & PRINT: Automated Processing of contracts, Forms, and Mailing Lists

WRITE, EDIT, & PRINT: The Word Processing—Phototypesetting Interface

These two volumes add eight more programs to **The Word Worker ®** system to provide the most extensive treatment of word processing available at any price.

Alexander for the IBM PC & PCjr — A word processing program that is extended to include characters not found in conventional systems. This program may be used for English, Spanish, French, German, Italian, Greek, Hebrew, Russian, typesetting "pi" characters, scientific & math notation, and music composition. It can be used with dot matrix and daisywheel printers as well as phototypesetting systems.

MAILING LIST and/or ORDER FORM

Please place me on your mailing list for future releases including:
- ☐ "WRITE, EDIT, & PRINT: Automated Processing of Contracts, Forms, and Mailing Lists"
- ☐ "WRITE, EDIT, & PRINT: The Word Processing—Phototypesetting Interface"
- ☐ "Alexander" Multilingual Word Processing, Scientific Notation, & Music Composition for the IBM PC & PCjr
- ☐ Additional titles for my computer which is: _______________________________

Date_______________________

Qty.

Computer Programming for the Compleat Idiot:
Microsoft Basic Edition

____ Copies Cloth	ISBN 0-932538-11-8	$18.95 __________
____ Copies Paper	ISBN 0-932538-12-6	$10.95 __________

Computer Programming for the Compleat Idiot:
The IBM PC & PCjr Edition

____ Copies Cloth	ISBN 0-932538-13-4	$18.95 __________
____ Copies Paper	ISBN 0-932538-14-2	$10.95 __________

WRITE, EDIT, & PRINT: Word Processing with Personal Computers

____ Copies Paper	ISBN 0-932538-06-1	$24.95 __________

WRITE, EDIT, & PRINT with **The Word Worker® Disk**

____ Disks for the IBM PC & PCjr	ISBN 0-932538-56-8	$49.95 __________
____ Disks for the Commodore 64 & PET/CBM	ISBN 0-932538-59-2	$49.95 __________
____ Disks for the Apple II & IIe	ISBN 0-932538-58-4	$49.95 __________
____ Disks for the TRS-80 I & III	ISBN 0-932538-60-6	$49.95 __________
____ Disks for the IBM-Compatible MS-DOS	ISBN 0-932538-57-6	$49.95 __________

CA Sales Tax* _____________

Shipping ($1.50)** _____________

TOTAL __________

All orders must be prepaid.
* CA residents add 6% Sales Tax
** $1.50 Shipping Charge on Individual Orders

I have enclosed a check/money order for $ _____________________________
Charge to my ☐ Master Card   ☐ Visa

Card # _______________________________   Expiration Date ________

Name ____

Address ____

_______________________________________   Zip __________

Mail Orders To:
DESIGN ENTERPRISES OF SAN FRANCISCO
P.O. Box 14695-I
San Francisco, CA 94114

Colophon

The cover art and design and the text design are by Mark Ong,
Berkeley, California.

The display type is Bookman Lite, the text type is Times Roman,
and the program listings are Helvetica.

Text entry was done on an IBM Personal Computer using The Word
Worker® Extended Writing, Printing, and Editing Programs.

Typesetting was done with an IBM PCjr using The Word Worker®
Typesetting Page Makeup and Telecommunication Programs to drive a
Compugraphic Jr. Typesetting System.

The printing is by Delta Lithograph Company, Van Nuys, California.

The binding of the case bound books is by Stauffer Edition Binding,
Monterey Park, California